I.O. Evans Studies
in the Philosophy and Criticism of Literature
ISSN 0271-9061
Number Sixteen

I0152186

The Dance of Consciousness

Enlightenment in Modern Literature

by

Douglas A. Mackey

BORGO PRESS / WILDSIDE PRESS

www.wildsidepress.com

* * * * * * * *

Library of Congress Cataloging-in-Publication Data

Mackey, Douglas A., 1947-
 The dance of consciousness : enlightenment in modern literature / by
Douglas A. Mackey.
  p. cm. — (I.O. Evans studies in the philosophy and criticism of
literature, ISSN 0271-9061 ; no. 16)
 Includes bibliographical references (p.) and index.
 ISBN 0-89370-305-2 (cloth). — ISBN 0-89370-405-9 (pbk.)
 1. Literature, Modern—20th century—History and criticism. 2. Consciousness in literature. I. Title. II. Series: I.O. Evans studies in the
philosophy & criticism of literature ; no. 16.
PN731.M33 1994   94-27641
809'.933384—dc20   CIP

TABLE OF CONTENTS

PREFACE

This book was substantially written in 1977–78. I would venture to say that in publishing it now, over fifteen years later, my general approach remains valid. Several important works have since appeared linking higher states of consciousness to literature: among them, Courtney Johnson's *Henry James and the Evolution of Consciousness,* Rhoda Orme-Johnson's "A Unified Field Theory of Literature," and William S. Haney's *Literary Theory and Sanskrit Poetics.* (Coincidentally, Haney discusses *The Crying of Lot 49* and *Ulysses,* as do I.) His focus is to interpret the extreme relativism of deconstructionism in the light of the timeless aesthetics of Vedic tradition. In so doing he has, I think, obviated any need I might have to address the peculiarities of contemporary literary theory.

The system of seven states of consciousness, as articulated by Maharishi Mahesh Yogi, is at the basis of this book. Though most religions have the idea of higher states of consciousness inherent in their mystical traditions, it is beyond the scope of my study to try to correlate them. I use Maharishi's system because it is the most simple, comprehensive, and profound one that I am aware of. However, Maharishi himself has implied that it is more of a beginner's map to the territory of higher consciousness rather than a schema to be rigidly insisted upon. In that spirit, I will happily agree that the assignment of specific literary works to specific states of consciousness is an arbitrary exercise, which I have done purely to enhance appreciation of both the works and the subtle patterns embedded in them.

Higher states of consciousness in relation to the fields of transpersonal psychology and quantum physics have been the focus of many books in recent years. My original plan was to touch on these correspondences in this book, because it is significant that present-day scientists have been so instrumental in helping the world break out of the materialist paradigm with which science itself has hypnotized us for centuries. I found that I could not do these ideas justice by peripheral references, and that my main argument lost focus in the process. Thus I will only refer the reader to such books as Stanislav Grof's *The Holotropic Mind,* Ken Wilber's *The Spectrum of Consciousness,* Alexander and Langer's *Higher Stages of Human Development,* and Anit Goswami's *The Self-Aware Universe,* among many excellent works on these subjects.

My debt to Maharishi Mahesh Yogi is obvious and overriding. In addition, I would like to acknowledge the help of Dr. Margaret Butler, Elizabeth Morrison, Dr. James Nourse, Dr. John Taber, Douglas Taylor, Laurie Ward, and Geoff Yarbrough for reading and commenting on various sections of the manuscript.

Douglas A. Mackey
June, 1994

Chapter 1

INVITATION TO THE DANCE

When you look at a painting or read a great work of literature for the first time, you see the tip of an iceberg. An immense subjectivity seethes beneath its surface, vibrating, yearning to be born again in you, if you will receive it. When you do, the work becomes translucent, revealing its crystalline depths. You gaze into the gap between two distant worlds—your mind and the artist's. Then the work becomes transparent and duality dissolves. The original creative energy streams into you.

That is the experience drawing us to art. It gives us a glimpse of the spaces beyond conscious awareness. It speaks in a tongue slightly unfamiliar and yet somehow native to our deepest souls. We recognize something in it that is in us. This is the sense, in picking up the book of an author we love, of going home.

Art should be judged as to whether or not it expands consciousness. If a certain book, song, or sculpture actually raises and refines your awareness, exhilarates and refreshes you, and bathes you with creative energy, then it may be considered "good." If it does this to enough people over a long period of time, then it may be accorded greatness.

The world as we know it is structured by our consciousness. Consciousness is a *substance;* literally, it "stands under" all things. We see as much as we are capable of seeing, and that capability is a function of our level of consciousness. When the level of consciousness rises, so does the level of reality that we perceive.

This does not mean that objects of perception are not really there. It is just that they are made of the substance of consciousness. We shape these objects according to our lights, but others may shape them differently, because the structure of the perceived world reflects the structure of the mind that perceives it. As infinite as the possibilities for perception is the field on which all these differences dance—and that field we shall call *pure consciousness.* The higher levels of consciousness we shall be exploring in this book all have pure consciousness at their basis.

I borrow Maharishi Mahesh Yogi's delineation of seven levels of consciousness, distinguished by characteristic patterns of mental and physical functioning. The first two levels are *deep sleep* and *dreaming,* commonly experienced by everyone. In deep sleep there is no mental activity but simply consciousness in a state of complete inertness. Nothing can be experienced. Dreaming is a more advanced state than deep sleep; there is some vague, illusory mental activity. But the subordinate status of that level of reality immediately becomes apparent when we awake.

A work of literature may depict sleep and dreaming but usually only within the context of a state of consciousness beyond them. For example, we shall see that August Strindberg in *A Dream Play* is concerned with the waking state of consciousness and uses the dream state as a metaphor to reveal the real nature of the waking state.

The third state of consciousness, the *waking state,* is the ordinary conscious functioning level of daily life. But in comparison to higher states, one is not really awake in it. In works by Beckett, Strindberg, and Pirandello that we shall analyze, the waking state is seen as a level of absurdity, illusion, and suffering. The reason is that in this state, consciousness is overshadowed by the objects of perception. Ordinarily, people define their existence in terms of the content of their thoughts. If they are able to think, they conclude that they exist. *Cogito, ergo sum* is very much the logic of the waking state. At this level, one is a slave to one's perceptions; one's true subjective nature is overshadowed by the object one perceives. The self is not known in itself and can only be defined in relation to external circumstances. Like everything else in the changing, relative world, the self seems finite, bounded, and transitory.

It is only in the fourth state of consciousness, *transcendental consciousness,* that one realizes what pure consciousness is. The process of meditation involves following a thought to its source in pure consciousness. As a wave settles down and becomes one with the sea, so the conscious awareness finds itself settling down to an ocean of unbounded awareness. The essential Self is realized as pure intelligence and infinite energy in a state of lively potentiality. This condition is called transcendental because it is beyond thought. Yet it is also the very source and substance of thought.

The fourth state is absolute. It never changes, it is always there, but unless we know how to become aware of it, life must remain shrouded in the boundaries of the first three relative states of consciousness, and the absolute Self will not be known. Ignorance—literally, the act of ignoring—is the only thing separating any human being from the bliss of transcendental consciousness.

Knowledge of the true nature of the Self can be found in every religious tradition. For Christ, the way and the truth and the life was the "I," the unbounded pure consciousness, the kingdom of heaven within. For Buddha, nirvana was the ultimate goal of life, and though he would not have that state with "Self," nirvana is the Absolute I equate here with pure consciousness. True religion emphasizes the desirability of Self-realization: it promises eternal happiness and freedom from the suffering characteristic of the waking state.

Great poets and artists have consistently pointed the way to transcendence—to transcendental consciousness and the states beyond it. Their expressions of transcendence tend to be highly individualistic and subjective—complementary to science, which uses objective methods to gain the highest possible knowledge and put it to work. Yet the artist, by representing the world as he or she sees it, filtered through a deep awareness of Self, touches the universal level in every person. The artist plumbs the subjective to its infinite source, while the scientist finds ways and means of following the galaxies to their origin beyond space and time, and of locating the source of life in every cell of a flower's petal.

The "experience" of transcendental consciousness is in a sense not an experience because there is no object of experience. It is simply consciousness without an object: the state of pure being. Yet in that being there is a lively potentiality like the still surface of a pond that has not been disturbed into ripples: "It is the revelation of the Self, in the Self, by the Self."[1]

C. G. Jung, Ingmar Bergman, and Thomas Pynchon have pointed very strongly towards the transcendental state in their work, as we shall see. They use the metaphor of the Quest to dramatize the innate human need to go beyond the ever-changing field of the relative world and discover the absolute, pure nature of the Self.

In the boundlessness of transcendental consciousness, there is but one thing lacking: boundaries. There is no object of perception: no people, no trees, no houses, not even any thoughts. But in the fifth state, *cosmic consciousness,* relative perceptions coexist with the transcendental state. One sees, hears, and senses as completely as in the waking state, but unlike the waking state, in cosmic consciousness the object of perception never overshadows the pure nature of the Self. One is fully conscious inside, whether sleeping, dreaming, or waking, twenty-four hours a day. This paradoxical state (how can one be asleep yet awake?) is one of "enlightenment," a condition of life naturally arrived at through repeated exposure to transcendental consciousness. We shall be considering Juan Ramón Jiménez, Alexander Scriabin, and D. H. Lawrence as modern prophets of this level of enlightenment.

When the Absolute is established in the awareness as an ever-present reality, the subjective sphere attains maximum evolution. The objective world now has a chance to rise to fullness. Because knowledge is structured in consciousness, we can really begin to understand and appreciate the world when the full range of the mind's potentialities is available. The sixth state, *God consciousness,* is the refinement of perceptions on the basis of cosmic consciousness until objects are apprehended at their most subtle, or celestial, level. Man does not become God here, but he is able to perceive the creation from the standpoint of the creator and thereby appreciate the supreme values of relative life. We shall read Hart Crane and Rainer Maria Rilke as exponents of this glorification of experience.

Even in God consciousness, however, there is duality. The separation between absolute Self and the relative world, realized in cosmic consciousness, continues here, although the gap lessens as the subtlest values of the relative open up to the senses. The evolution of consciousness to the seventh state, *Unity consciousness,* resolves this duality altogether. It is as if the Self has grown so great that it over-flows the subjective realm and completely permeates the object. The experience of Unity is expressed in the Vedic aphorism *Tat tvam asi,* "thou art That." The house, the tree, the other person, is seen and enjoyed and valued *as oneself.* The relative world is seen ultimately as *maya,* a veil over the Absolute, with each individual wave on the sea of life perceived in essence as unindividuated water. Unity consciousness, then, upholds the full value of both relative and Absolute, but the Absolute, or pure consciousness, is found everywhere as the fundamental reality. We shall examine works by Robert M. Pirsig, James Joyce, and John Cowper Powys as representing a unified view of life paralleling this highest level of consciousness.

This brief summary of the seven states of consciousness is abstract, but as we survey specific works of literature, these states should acquire more human coloring.

I can't speculate whether the authors mentioned above were themselves in higher states of consciousness. It may very well be that great artists and writers through the ages have had at least glimpses of transcendental consciousness, to say nothing of the states beyond it. But there is no way to know for sure that is the case, even in the rare cases (such as Wordsworth) where we have personal reports. And it is not necessary for the purposes of this study.

A work of literature can reveal a higher state of consciousness in several different ways. First, a character can be portrayed as being in one of these states, as in D. H. Lawrence's *The Escaped Cock,* where Christ's resurrection takes on the meaning of an entry into cosmic consciousness. Secondly, a work may suggest higher consciousness through symbol and archetype; an example of this is the castle that blossoms into a chrysanthemum at the end of Strindberg's *A Dream Play.* Thirdly, the work may imply a higher state by its very form, as *Ulysses,* through its unitive structure, suggests Unity consciousness.

Symbol, myth, and archetype are especially relevant to the ensuing analyses. As these terms are often used interchangeably, I shall try to differentiate them in terms of their relationship to consciousness.

A *symbol* is any image that points beyond its literal form to more abstract levels. It doesn't have a single, concrete referent as a "sign" does; it does not merely stand for something else. A symbol usually evokes a complex of emotional and intellectual associations, and is ambiguous by nature.

As Aniela Jaffé notes, "symbol" derives from *symbolon,* the broken coin whose halves fit together precisely and is shared between two parting friends as a representation of their essential unity.[2] A verbal symbol is a window on the Absolute. Its purpose is to restore the broken link between a man's conscious mind and his transcendental nature by taking him from the level of the concrete image through levels of greater abstraction towards the ultimate abstraction of transcendental consciousness.

The *archetype* is a universal symbol, a form or pattern that has such a great degree of abstraction that it tends to be repeated in different times and places with many different colorings. Leopold Bloom and Odysseus are cases of the archetypal explorer-hero who undertakes a quest for home. But they themselves are not archetypes: they are manifestations of the archetype.

There is some confusion between the terms myth and archetype. Jung points out that an archetype is "an irrepresentable unconscious, pre-existent form," "empty and purely formal," a possibility not filled in by content.[3] A myth, on the other hand, is a manifestation of the archetype, its content determined by cultural and environmental influences.

A *myth* is a story, old or new, that tells the tale of the expansion of consciousness. Not only ancient legends of gods and heroes, but modern works as well, can be seen as mythic when they strike this universal chord. It may seem strange now to call *Waiting for Godot* a myth, but in five thousand years it may be quite natural to do so.

As myths are stories about the evolution and fulfillment of consciousness, the higher states of consciousness are always implicit in them. The Oedipus myth is a symbolic tale of the transition to cosmic consciousness. At the beginning of Sophocles' play, Oedipus is the most accomplished of men, yet plunged into ignorance of his own Self, a condition symbolized by his lack of knowledge about the true identity of his parents. When the revelation of his incest and patricide comes, it is agonizingly painful to bear and he gouges out his eyes. But this act, purely tragic on the surface, symbolizes a deeper accession to wisdom. Oedipus finds that by withdrawing his senses from the outer world he gains a higher vision and becomes a seer and a prophet. Like all great tragedy, *Oedipus Rex* conveys a sense of transcendence and victory through surrender to the necessity of change in the relative sphere. If the story of a man's painful defeat is all that we derive from *Oedipus*, then we have not penetrated its mythic level.

Joseph Campbell has postulated the one great archetypal pattern of the "monomyth" as the essential root myth in which all stories have their source. Simply stated, the monomyth is the Quest or hero-journey: "A hero ventures forth from the world of common day into a region of supernatural wonder: fabulous forces are there encountered and a decisive victory is won: the hero comes back from this mysterious adventure with the power to bestow boons on his fellow man."[4] Campbell designates these three stages of the monomyth as Separation, Initiation, and Return.

The structure of the monomyth contains all the possibilities for the evolution of consciousness. In meditation, we leave the relative behind, dip into the Absolute, then return to the world with increased energy and intelligence. This brief journey encompasses Separation (indeed, the ultimate separation of Absolute and relative), Initiation (the union of the conscious mind with its own essential nature in transcendental consciousness), and Return (with the boon of an enriched awareness of life, which serves as a basis for positive action in society). This natural expansion of consciousness is thus reflected in the most essential pattern to be found in myth and literature.

When a meditating individual, by virtue of many exposures to transcendental consciousness, stabilizes cosmic consciousness, the possibility of further transcendence is ruled out. Once transcendental consciousness is established as a permanent reality, the Absolute is ever-present and there is no longer any need to transcend the relative to get there. However, cosmically conscious people find themselves in a state of radical separation from the phenomenal world. They know themselves to be eternal, but outside them matter is in a state of perpetual flux. Though free, blissful, and infinite, they are separate from the world, and this duality must be resolved by a further evolution of consciousness.

If cosmic consciousness represents Separation, God consciousness represents Initiation, and Unity consciousness, Return. The Initiation stage of the monomyth, which may include such events as the hero's union with the mother-goddess or atonement with the father-creator, is symbolic of the godlike refinement of perception that occurs in God consciousness, and of the harmony of the individual with the forces of nature that comes in that state. Campbell recognizes the boon gained at this stage as "intrinsically . . . an expansion of consciousness and therewith of being."[5]

The Return phase corresponds to Unity consciousness because here the division that was created in cosmic consciousness is entirely mended. As the mythic hero returns to his homeland with the boon, so the evolving person brings the boon of his or her enlightenment "home" to the outside world, investing everything seen with the infinite nature of the Self. The world glows with the very light by which he or she is conscious.

Campbell beautifully describes the entire process of evolution of consciousness from transcendental consciousness to Unity, although he does not use those terms:

> This is the stage of Narcissus looking into the pool, of the
> Buddha sitting contemplative under the tree, but it is not

the ultimate goal; it is a requisite step, but not the end. The aim is not to see, but to realize that one is, that essence [transcendental consciousness]; then one is free to wander as that essence in the world [cosmic consciousness]. Furthermore: the world too is of that essence. The essence of oneself and the essence of the world: these two are one. Hence separateness, withdrawal, is no longer necessary. Wherever the hero may wander, whatever he may do, he is ever in the presence of his own essence—for he has the perfected eye to see. There is no separateness [Unity consciousness].[6]

Thus the monomyth is recapitulated in the evolution of the individual consciousness in each meditation and in the totality of one's spiritual growth.

The ultimate symbolic value of the mythic narrative is in its relevance to an individual's evolution. The hero is Everyman in the process of expanding his awareness. His story is our story.

Consciousness is a dimension in the study of literature which is all too often totally ignored—consciousness, that is, in the sense of the unbounded, unmanifest Self that is at the basis of personal and cosmic existence. Consciousness in its more limited "waking state" aspect as ego-awareness and so on is simply too insubstantial a basis for serious discussion of great works.

Higher states of consciousness are becoming more widely known about and experienced. These archetypal modalities of consciousness are innate in every individual and may be identified in the art and literature of all ages. It makes no difference in what time period we locate them, but I have chosen representative works from the twentieth century. The art and literature of this period, whatever verdict history will render about its ultimate artistic value, is replete with indications of humankind's evolution into a new paradigm in which enlightenment is understood and accepted as every person's birthright.

Chapter 2

ABSURDITY

Samuel Beckett: *Waiting for Godot*
Luigi Pirandello: *Six Characters in Search of an Author*
August Strindberg: *A Dream Play*

The wasteland has long been a symbol of spiritual stagnation, from Dante's darkling wood and Bunyan's Vanity Fair to Blake's Ulro and Eliot's "unreal city." But in a century in which society, up until now, has seemed to drift farther and farther from its traditional sources of spiritual sustenance, the wasteland image has never been so pertinent. As Joseph Campbell explains, the wasteland is a landscape of spiritual death that is waiting for the Desired Knight to restore the lost living waters from the "inexhaustible source."[1] Societies with a viable traditional mythology use ritual symbolic forms—artifacts, dances, tales, prayers, masks—to help them maintain a connection to that source of fertility. But when the symbols of a culture are vitiated, individuals must create their own. The peculiar burden of the modern artist has been to invent a new mythology through rediscovering ancient myths and applying archetypal structures to contemporary life.

Broadly speaking, the wasteland stands for the waking state of consciousness. We know from experience that the waking state is not always a wasteland. It has its joys as well as sorrows. But when we consider that compared to the higher states, this supposed normalcy is sheerest ignorance, the waking state is indeed a desolate, feckless, arid condition. The characters in the three plays by Beckett, Pirandello, and Strindberg have realized the predicament of being lost in a wasteland, and they are trying to get out of it.

Beckett's *Waiting for Godot* (1954) is a classical expression of the modern preoccupation with the wasteland. The stage is bare except for a low mound and a tree, which, though it appears dead in the first act, sprouts a few leaves by the second. The two principal characters, Vladimir and Estragon, are ragged hoboes. They fight, make up, play games to pass the time, laugh and cry, try to remember what happened

15

the day before, abuse each other, embrace each other, tell gross jokes, philosophize, sing, howl, sear, and above all, wait. As an audience of San Quentin prisoners readily perceived, the pair are in prison though not physically constrained. Imprisonment is a state of mind. Vladimir and Estragon are not bound in space or time, but their mind-forged manacles make them think they are.

They cannot leave the stage, though they try many times, because they must wait for Godot, who is their salvation. Each day they expect him, and each day he sends a boy with the message that he will come tomorrow. This leaves the two tramps in a state of indefinite suspension. The only thing that keeps them from committing suicide is the hope that Godot will come and deliver them in some way from the meaninglessness of their existence. This tenuous link to Something Else, we are given to understand, is an illusion. Godot will never come.

Because their destiny is postponed indefinitely, the present for them is a great, endless void, as empty as the stage. One day is like another, and because there is so little to distinguish the days, the tramps have a great deal of difficulty remembering the past.

> Vladimir: The tree, look at the tree.
> Estragon: Was it not there yesterday?
> Vladimir: Yes of course it was there. Do you not
> remember? We nearly hanged ourselves from it. But
> you wouldn't. Do you not remember?
> Estragon: You dreamt it.
> Vladimir: Is it possible you've forgotten already?
> Estragon: That's the way I am. Either I forget
> immediately or I never forget.[2]

The twentieth century experience has been for many people one of fragmentation: a feeling of being cut off from the living traditions of the past and of being deprived of possibility for regeneration in the future. Vladimir and Estragon are representative of this condition. Beckett implies that all people, stripped of their material and intellectual pretensions, reduce to this: tramps, clowns, in an indeterminate place at an indeterminate time, utterly ignorant of the meaning of their existence and on the edge of despair.

Beckett's vision is not very encouraging, but in his attempt to reduce life to its bare essentials, he succeeds in conveying the reality of the waking state of consciousness. His message and that of the existentialists was an important one: if we face life honestly, we must admit that we are ignorant, our senses are deficient and inadequate to interpret reality, our sanity is an illusion of stability fostered by the time-wasting games we play. For only when the waking state is seen as limited does the motivation come to search for transcendence.

The play takes place against the background of a terrifying void. The two tramps stick together for fear of loneliness. They are incapable of leaving each other for long, or being silent:

> Estragon: In the meantime let us try and converse
> calmly, since we are incapable of keeping silent.
> Vladimir: You're right, we're inexhaustible.
> Estragon: It's so we won't think.
> Vladimir: We won't have that excuse.
> Estragon: It's so we won't hear.
> Vladimir: We have our reasons.
> Estragon: All the dead voices.
> Vladimir: They make a noise like wings.
> Estragon: Like leaves.
> Vladimir: Like sand.
> Estragon: Like leaves.[3]

Their conversation itself is barely on the fringe of meaningfulness. It threatens to lull them into amnesia and silence again. The void which is always menacing them permeates their words. The frequent repetitions, as here of "leaves," creates a hypnotic, rustling effect. The monotony of their chatter is the drone of the very void they are trying to forget.

From the standpoint of the bounded waking state, the idea of infinity is often frightening. One remembers the cabin boy Pip in *Moby-Dick* who was left to float alone in the wide ocean for hours, and who went insane because his tiny individuality was engulfed by the infinitude of sky and sea. There is something in the human psyche that does love a wall. The boundaries of things as we have become accustomed to them are reassuring. If they changed all the time, we would have to reorient ourselves constantly, and that would be difficult and possibly unpleasant.

There is also something in us that forces us to wait for Godot, even if all reason tells us it is hopeless. It is the nature of life to grow, and our consciousness, like a green plant, must continue to thrust outward in new shoots. We are not content with the indefinite perpetuation of things as they are. Reality, no matter how lush, will deteriorate to a wasteland if the root of that reality, the consciousness that perceives it, is not watered and renewed.

The tramps' environment is an exteriorization of their spiritually bankrupt state of consciousness. So also is their God, Godot. He is an old man with a white beard, the conventional anthropomorphic patriarchal divinity, an image of wisdom, justice, and transcendence. But he is so transcendent as to be inaccessible. The tramps wait in vain, and they cannot go to him because they do not know how or where to look.

From the human point of view, Godot is irrational. He beats the servant boy who tends the sheep but not the one who minds the goats. He sends daily messages that he will come, but he never does. He seems like a master comedian whose whole purpose is to make fools of those who wait for him. In Greek tragedy as well, the gods often behave inexplicably: Apollo apparently initiates Oedipus's tragedy by inciting him to go to Thebes with the prophecy of his patricide and incest. Tragedy is by nature mysterious in its results. One feels that the characters' destiny, happy or sad, has been worked out, perhaps with a little help from above, and that it is somehow right in the total picture of the world of the play. Vladimir and Estragon's tragedy is that they fail to transcend the wasteland of their lives; they seem doomed to reenact over and over the trivialities and banalities of their daily routine. Estragon will forever be beaten at night (or dream he is); Vladimir will forever be reminding Estragon why they are waiting; the two will forever be attempting or contemplating suicide and not be able to go through with it.

In their failure is also their victory. They have tried to live. They are at least aware of their need for Godot. Vladimir says: "We are not saints, but we have kept our appointment. How many people can boast as much?" Estragon replies, "Billions."[4] There are two other characters, Pozzo and Lucky, who do not know they have an appointment to keep. They are the archetypal master and slave, bound to each other by a rope, destroying each other with mutual dependence.

Unlike the tramps, whose companionship helps to sustain them, Pozzo and Lucky's relationship is sado-masochistic. Whereas Vladimir and Estragon's condition is quite the same in Act II as in Act I, Lucky and Pozzo's is greatly deteriorated. Pozzo is superior, greedy, abusive, and patronizing in Act I; he is given to false poeticizing and sentimental truisms. These affectations are stripped from him in Act II after he

18

has been struck blind. His words are heartfelt now in his genuine despair:

> One day, is that not enough for you, one day he went dumb, one day I went blind, one day we'll go deaf, one day we were born, one day we shall die, the same day, the same second, is that not enough for you? *(Calmer)* They give birth astride of a grave, the light gleams an instant, then it's night once more.[5]

Pozzo's sins have finally come home to roost. After tyrannizing Lucky, he is now tyrannized by time. Life seems infinitely short to him, an instant of light in a night of unconsciousness and pain. The tramps at least have the reassurance of continuity and the hope of escaping the prison cell of their lives. They are capable of love, of a human relationship, and that is a great comfort against the void. And they do have their ultimate *raison d'être:* Godot.

Lucky is not so lucky. He is Pozzo's slave, a groveling idiot with a festering sore and a rope around his neck. Yet he speaks the most eloquent words in the play in a long lunatic babble, his only departure from silence. The gist of it is that man suffers and God is either uninterested or unable to help him, a message that is corroborated in the play by Godot's inaccessibility. Lucky is apparently unconscious of any meaning in his speech; the dazzling verbal brilliance he displays is accidental, his "wisdom" buried in a chaotic mass of absurd allusions and digressions. In the second act he is struck dumb, deprived of even the expression of his madness.

Pozzo and Lucky are subject to entropy. Their external condition degenerates and finally most closely matches their subhuman psychological state. Pozzo could never really see so he loses his sight; Lucky could never really think rationally so he loses the ability to speak. As Blake put it, "Standing water breeds pestilence."

In comparison to Pozzo and Lucky's stagnation, Vladimir and Estragon's waiting is a positive act. They cannot *do* anything to find Godot, it seems. If they are to contact him at all it will be by culturing receptivity and patience. They are in the painful process of learning not-doing.

It might be departing somewhat from the intention of the author to speculate that in fact Godot will eventually come for the holy fools Vladimir and Estragon. The bare tree has sprouted a few leaves by Act

II, suggesting that some slow growth is going on. (When you have nothing, even a little is a lot.) This reawakened fertility in the tree implies that Vladimir and Estragon's wait is not altogether futile. But Godot will not appear as they envision him, nor will he come from the direction they expect him.

Within the context of the play, Godot remains offstage. Within the boundaries of the waking state, God also stays in the transcendent. Godot, a man with a white beard, symbolizes the inner guru, the intuitive intellect. He is an image of Vladimir and Estragon's higher self, unattainable as long as they look for him outside themselves.

In Beckett's play, the background void is an absolute, a continuity of nothingness, a silence whose voice is despair. And Godot is also negative, a cruel trickster. This is the point of view of the waking state of consciousness. But what if it were possible to take a different angle on that void and on Godot?

Waiting for Godot gives us the very beginning of a vision of possibilities. Despite its reputation as an utterly bleak play, it is as comic as it is tragic, and this especially comes through when we see it on the stage or read it with consciousness of its theatrical possibilities. Vladimir and Estragon are clowns with sad faces. Comedy is a compensation for their situation and a way of acceptance of their lives' essential limitation: that they must wait.

It is difficult to isolate any line in the play as either comic or tragic because almost everything is double-edged. For example the following exchange:

> Vladimir: But you can't go barefoot!
> Estragon: Christ did.
> Vladimir: Christ! What has Christ got to do with it?
> You're not going to compare yourself to Christ!
> Estragon: All my life I've compared myself to him.
> Vladimir: But where he lived it was warm, it was dry!
> Estragon: Yes. And they crucified quick.[6]

The thought of Estragon as a modern Christ is funny while containing a serious dimension, for Christ is alive within the frowsy hobo Estragon if he is anywhere at all. And Estragon thinks positively about crucifixion. It would mean the cessation of his wretched life. His *angst* throws a comic light on the original tragedy.

Walter Kerr maintains in *Tragedy and Comedy* that comedy is based on an acceptance of limitation and tragedy upon an attempt to expand freedom. *Waiting for Godot* is a fusion of the two modes because Vladimir and Estragon, in attempting to expand their freedom, must learn to accept the limiting factor of the existence—of waiting. This necessity is comic because the wait seems endless, pointless, and absurd, but it is also heroic and potentially tragic because their waiting is a positive holding action against the kind of entropy that Pozzo and Lucky represent. In *Godot* the waking state of consciousness is full of ambiguity, irrational by its own terms but comprehensible when viewed from outside.

When we know of the existence of higher states of consciousness, Beckett's play is not itself a doctrine of absurdity; it merely represents absurdity. But Beckett's theoretical statements about art do not indicate that he would sanction this view. He once defined his kind of art as "the expression that there is nothing to express, nothing with which to express, no power to express, no desire to express, together with the obligation to express."[7] Beckett seems to think that art should take the position that life is barren and accept it as such, rather than represent the barrenness without accepting it. For me, art must help one to transcend the barrenness. Despite Beckett's pessimistic philosophic utterances, in this play he succeeds in transcending the barren waking state by suffusing the tragic situation with comic detachment.

Beckett negates everything that he finds inessential and ends up with a basis for finding the real. When the play works on the stage, the audience can gain a satisfaction that the characters cannot—that of seeing through the characters' illusions. This is the beginning of a vision of renewal, just by virtue of the fact that the wasteland of the waking state of consciousness is shown for what it is—a condition of pure relativity, dependent upon mental conceptions of time and space. Though Beckett may claim he has nothing to express, the audience will not fail to make something of his expression. The play, like a Rorschach inkblot, will elicit as many different responses as there are people to view it. The "emptiness" of his vision is like a blank screen upon which anything can be projected. In a sense, Beckett provides us with an archetype and invites us to fill it in. The effect is that the archetypal wasteland and the archetypal characters who inhabit it—the clowns, the master and slave—come to life as they remind us of our own lives.

Beckett's play is filled with intentional ambiguities that express the paradoxical and fundamentally irrational nature of the waking state. We come to see life as something that cannot be comprehended from a purely material perspective. There is no justification for the fate and behavior of Vladimir and Estragon unless we accept that the transcendent power that they are waiting for is real, not an empty illusion; and that it is already beginning to manifest in their lives, from within.

Luigi Pirandello's *Six Characters in Search of an Author* (1921) also portrays people in a state of ignorance, who cannot see their way out of their complex problems. But it too gives the audience an opportunity to find relief. One of Pirandello's famous exercises on the theme of reality and illusion, this play instills in us a sense that we cannot trust our senses, and this feeling lingers well after we have left the theatre. Having shown the paradoxes implicit in our daily life, the author leads us towards a state of transcendence. Time after time he reminds us that life is like a play, thus giving us a transcendent distance on it.

The curtain opens on a theatrical company rehearsing a play—one by Pirandello, as a matter of fact. Immediately we are plunged into a multi-dimensional reality where mirrors reflect images from yet other mirrors. We are given the illusion that we are not seeing a mere play but rather the reality behind the making of a play. Heightened illusion produces heightened reality. Suddenly upon the set appear six uninvited guests: a man, his wife, his son, his step-daughter, and two young step-children, a boy and a girl. They identify themselves enigmatically as "characters" who have been conceived by an unknown author but have not been born into a work of art. So they ask the director of this company to let them live through his actors. Their compulsion is to have their drama played.

The father equates his status as Character with a kind of immortality:

> . . . a character can laugh even at death. He cannot die.
> The man, the writer, the instrument of the creation does
> not die. And to live forever, it does not need to have ex-
> traordinary gifts or to be able to work wonders. Who was
> Sancho Panza? Who was Don Abbondio? Yet they live
> eternally because—live germs as they were—they had the

fortune to find a fecundating matrix, a fantasy which
could raise and nourish them: make them live forever![8]

Like Coleridge's Ancient Mariner, who was compelled to seek out lis-
teners for his tale, reliving his frightful experience over and over, so
the six characters are compelled to seek out actors to complete their
being.

A sordid story is soon revealed: the father, many years before, had
sent his wife away to live with a man she loved. By that man she had
three children; her eldest son, however, was legitimate and remained
with the father. When the lover died, she and the children returned to
her husband, arousing the antipathy of this son. Also the father has
barely avoided bedding his own step-daughter during a period when
she was a prostitute. For that inadvertent indiscretion she continues to
berate him.

Without even attempting to play their drama, the Characters reveal
these facts through their conflicts, and all the Actors in the theatrical
company are completely absorbed by this unconscious performance.
But when the Actors attempt to dramatize the story, it doesn't approach
the genuineness of emotion of the "reality" they have just witnessed.
The Characters have more reality than the Actors, even though pre-
sumably they are fictional and do not actually exist. Compared to them,
the Actors are shallow and superficial. Art imitates life very badly here.

In the context of the play we are watching, the Actors are "real"
and the Characters are "art." The Characters' reality is illusory. Yet
when life attempts to imitate art, it seems to be less substantial than the
imaginal reality. This is the central paradox of the play: when illusion
seems more real than reality, reality becomes illusion.

The Actors' profession is in making illusions, yet when confronted
with real illusions in the persons of the Characters, they are inadequate
to represent them. The Characters are much more convincing in por-
traying their own parts. Paradoxically, they are living from a deeper
plane of real feeling than the actors who are supposedly rooted in reality.

The appearance of the Characters shatters the conventional framework of reality and illusion. From their point of view, they are more
real than anybody else. As the father explains, for "real" people life is
always changing, and what is reality today will seem like illusion tomorrow. But for the Characters the situation is different:

Our reality doesn't change: it can't change! It can't be other than what it is, because it is already fixed for ever. It's terrible. Ours is an immutable reality which should make you shudder when you approach us if you are really conscious of the fact that your reality is a mere transitory and fleeting illusion, taking this form today and that tomorrow, according to the conditions, according to your will, your sentiments, which in turn are controlled by an intellect that shows them to you today in one manner and tomorrow . . . who knows how? . . . Illusions of reality represented in this fatuous comedy of life that never ends, nor can ever end![9]

The father goes on to speak of the independence of the Character from his creator: the Character can be imagined by other minds in other places than the creator ever thought of putting him, and thus he can acquire new meanings.

The father perceives that any "reality" in a state of perpetual flux is not worthy of the name. Relative life, if viewed from a relative standpoint, will always shift and be found in new aspects without any stable factor of continuity. But the Characters, whose reality never changes, are in an even worse position because they cannot grow. They are doomed to replay the drama of their lives endlessly. It is hell for them. Their unchanging "reality" is a cruel prison where there is no transcendence of problems and neuroses.

Pirandello's paradoxes display two characteristics of the waking state of consciousness. First, one man's waking state reality is seen by another man as illusion. Second, since the surface values of relative life are constantly changing, there can be no stable point of reference in the relative. If one attempts to fix such a point, one will suffer, as do the Characters, who are locked into their behavior patterns.

If there is an absolute in the relative, it can only be that change is inevitable and continuous. This is the main point that Pirandello wants to make about human personality: that we are always changing, that we are many people. We wear masks, presenting different faces at different times and utterly transforming ourselves to accommodate each situation. It is an illusion that we are one personality. No single point of view of a person is adequate to encompass the many faces. The father pleads, for example, not to be judged on the basis of his moment of indiscretion with the step-daughter; that isolated incident should not brand him as a lecher.

The Characters are fixed unnaturally in their limited roles; they are not free to change fluidly like "real" people. Their destiny is pre-determined: "We act that role for which we have been cast, that role which we are given in life."[10] By implication, this is the human condition: we are creatures of habit and unconsciously play and replay the same behavior patterns, acting under the illusion of free will. The six Characters can do nothing to avert their fate, though they are fully aware of it. They have no free will, and neither do the actors, if they only knew it.

The metaphor of life as a stage play in which man must act a pre-determined part according to script was a favorite of Shakespeare's in the famous passages from *As You Like It, Macbeth,* and *The Tempest* ("All the world's a stage," "life's but a walking shadow, a poor player," "and like this insubstantial pageant faded"). Pirandello adds a twist to this theme that life is a web of illusion, a charade. He implies that art, man's subcreation, is a higher reality than the primary creation. Art speaks the truth about life; it enables us to stand apart from life and see it as a play. Thereby are we liberated from the constraints of our narrow range of waking consciousness.

Nobody in *Six Characters* is free. The Characters know they have no chance of escaping their fate but are compelled to act it out anyway. They are tragic; they try to burst their limitations and cannot. But simultaneously one of them, the father, displays the comic vision. He is the stock character that Pirandello uses in many of his plays as his mouthpiece. The father has a transcendent detachment towards his condition and accepts the limitations of the human lot—the relativity of different points of view, the indeterminacy of truth, the illusory fabric of waking reality. He mocks the Director and Actors who are not aware that they too are Characters.

In another Pirandello play, *Right You Are If You Think You Are,* the character Laudisi formulates this definitive statement of the nature of the waking state of consciousness: "What is truth? Truth does not exist: truth we have in ourselves: truth is the representation that each of us makes of it."[11] But what if there were an individual who did not see only shadows? What if there were one who had emerged from the cave of ignorance and could see in the clear light of day? Pirandello does not discuss this eventuality. But he points the way by saying, "truth we have in ourselves." The ultimate reference point has to be ourselves, because the self is the only continuity in a universe of flux. Pirandello, however, asserts that the integrity of the self is illusory, that we are really a mass of contradictory selves, though one of the selves may have the upper hand over the others. The identification with a limited aspect of self, the ego or conscious thinking mind, to the extent that it overshadows the true Self, is a mistake of the waking state of consciousness.

Pirandello explores the implications of the aphorism "Knowledge is structured in consciousness" with reference to the waking state. Though none of his characters are able to transcend their relative viewpoints, except the father to some extent on the purely intellectual level, the audience is given an aesthetic experience that enables them to transcend theirs.

Perhaps the six Characters think that by replaying their past they can break through the formal limitations on their freedom. And perhaps they are right. Their search for an author is a search for their source, the guiding intelligence which has determined their lives. The truth cannot be without, it can only be within them, so their search is a desire for the source of thought, the pure consciousness that originates all action and is the ultimate "free will" directing us on the tortuous byways of life.

This invisible author is the Godot, the ancient Greek *daimon*—which, as Marco Pallis has noted, originally meant "the intuitive intelligence indwelling at the heart of every being and especially of man, the immanent grace about which Christ said 'the kingdom of heaven is within you.' "[12] Pirandello's Characters do not achieve their goal, but they are on the right track. Their acting out of the play of their lives is a ritual, therapeutic purgation by which they hope to rise from the boundaries of the relative personality to the boundlessness of the true Self.

Pirandello conceived the "Life Force" as an indomitable purposive flow of change in all things—people, trees, stars. Opposed to this force is the Mask, the covering that people try to lay over the Life Force.[13] Identifying themselves with the Mask, or superficial personality, rather than with the Life Force—the deep, fluid, infinite potentiality of consciousness—they trade the glory of living from the level of the Author for the tenuous, joyless security of the Character's Mask.

In *Moby-Dick,* Ahab envisioned the White Whale's inscrutable brow as a mask, and announced his fanatical passion to "strike through the mask." This is a good definition of the tragic purpose: the hero denies his limitations and seeks to burst the constrictions on his aware-ness, the chains that make him a creature of the Mask rather than of the Life Force. It is no wonder that tragedy, in affirming the nature of life to evolve to higher levels, is considered by many to be nobler than comedy.

The six Characters, because they are too attached to their masks, fail as heroes. They cannot break out of their roles. A dull knife will not cut, and they are trying to transcend waking consciousness with the dull consciousness of the Mask itself. The only way to transcend is to take off the Mask.

Nevertheless, these Characters are nobler than the Actors in the play. By and large, the Actors are a shallow, egotistic lot, puffed up in their self-images as artists. Their Masks are even more opaque than those of the Characters. They have no conception of the need to strike through the Mask, because they aren't even aware that they are wearing Masks. The Actors are competent in their art but quite stupid con-cerning art's transcendent purpose: to reveal the phenomenal world, or "real life," as a mask over the Life Force, and to uncover the greater glory shining through the boundaries.

The six Characters, though they possess an immortality of a sort—they cannot change—yearn for another kind of immortality, that of being in contact with the indomitable flow of life. They seek to eschew the false absolute of the illusion of personality for the true Absolute of the Life Force. When they enter for the first time the Director asks them what they want; the Father replies, "We want to live." "For eter-nity?" is the ironic rejoinder. "No sir," replies the Father, "only for a moment . . . in you."[14] The immortality they seek is not indefinite con-tinuance in time, which could only perpetuate their present misery, but a transcendence of time altogether, a deliverance from the time-bound cyclical world into the Eternal Now.

The Characters do not find the fulfillment they seek. They are never born into real life and remain trapped in their world of illusion. They play out their final tragedy, in which the young boy drowns the baby sister, then shoots himself out of guilt for the sins of his parents. The melodramatic situation of the play-within-the-play approaches tragic dimensions, and the actors are stunned by this final stroke of reality in the midst of their activity of illusion-making. We in the audi-ence are stunned too. We have become involved with the Characters' story and forgotten that it is a fiction invented by an Author. But then the frame of *Six Characters,* the rehearsal of a play, is a fiction too, which we are even more likely to forget as we get into the inner story. The feeling that we take away from the theatre is that life itself is a multi-layered fabric of realities, colored by differing subjectivities and gripped only tenuously and fleetingly, the substance of the relative world seeming to melt away when we try to pin it down. This is the true nature of the waking state of consciousness: a play of shifting masks over the essential, unknowable reality.

If there is a "reality" worthy of its name, Pirandello implies, it must be non-changing. But the stasis of the Characters' roles is a false absolute: it is suspension in time, not transcendence of time. The play opens up towards transcendence, however, because it places the audience in a transcendent perspective. Art intensifies "real life" by representing its unreality, and when we can perceive this, we are set free from the bondage of the roles we play in life. Walter Starkie has beautifully described the sensation of being so transported by a Pirandello play:

> It is in these moments of internal silence when our soul divests itself of all our customary figments and our eyes become more acute and penetrating: we see ourselves in life and life in itself, as though we were stark naked; we feel a strange impression creep over us, as if in a flash a fresh reality was lit up for us, different to the one we normally see, a supreme reality that transcends human vision and human reason.[15]

If Pirandello's Characters have no way out of their webs of illusion, his audiences are not so unfortunate. In a good production of his play, we should have the experience of that "internal silence" that results when the intellect, suspended in its inability to explain the paradoxical relative world, rests and allows the experience of what is beyond ordinary awareness to flood in.

Godot and *Six Characters* make us entertain the idea of a transcendental reality by exposing the phenomenal world seen by waking consciousness as a spiritually barren place. Both Beckett and Pirandello imply that life as most know it is but a dream and that being truly alive means awaking from it. Strindberg gives this analogy its most classic formulation in *A Dream Play* (1902).

Strindberg attempted to replicate the sensation of a dream on stage by providing fast transitions from one scene to another with a setting flexible enough that no time would be occupied by scene changes. The scenery makes no pretense at being realistic; Strindberg despised the illusionist conventions of the nineteenth century stage. The time sequences are as fluid as the scene changes. For example, we see an Officer enter several times in the space of a few minutes, waiting at the door of his ideal woman, Miss Victoria, who does not emerge, and in that time he ages from a dashing young man to a broken old greybeard. The characters themselves are abstractions; despite their psychological veracity, they have a shadowy particularity, and seem as much types as individuals.

Strindberg's approach is non-realistic in one sense, but by breaking down conventional stage realism he pierces the surface level of mind which perceives time as linear and human beings as unchanging personae, static entities. He appeals to a subtler level of understanding and intuition, equally "real."

The play begins somewhere in the high heavens. The daughter of the god Indra is drifting down to earth; she is anxious to experience for herself the ways of men. She arrives before a castle, the central symbol of the work. It sits in the manured earth, growing steadily; a glazier is kept busy adding windows to the new stories. All the bizarre landscapes of the succeeding scenes are located within its walls.

Going inside the castle, the Daughter in her human incarnation of Agnes rouses the Officer from his imprisonment there, telling him, "It's your duty to find your way to the light." But he is trapped in his memories of an unhappy childhood—especially his guilt over having destroyed a copy of *The Swiss Family Robinson.* Agnes, however, is confident that "love conquers everything." Then follows a scene where the Officer seeks the beautiful Miss Victoria at her stage door, but his waiting is as futile as the tramps' for Godot.

Agnes, becoming more entangled in the cares of material existence, gets acquainted with a Lawyer, an embittered idealist. He offers her "the best of life and the worst," and she accepts, wanting "to know everything, to try everything." Their marriage soon turns into a nightmare: he likes cabbage, she detests it; she is an unfastidious housekeeper, and he cannot abide crooked candlesticks. Each suffers from what the other desires, but to avoid wars they agree to stifle themselves, to sacrifice, and to suppress their differences. The airlessness of the relationship is symbolized by the maid's continual pasting and sealing of the windows in their room.

The Officer reappears to whisk Agnes away to Fairhaven, a land of eternal "youth and happiness, children and flowers, singing and dancing, picnics and parties." But first they must pass through Foulstrand, a hell of pigsties, charred hills, and torture devices, where they witness the agonies of those who sought pleasure burning in carbolic acid. A Poet enters, walking with his eyes fixed on the stars but carrying a bucket of mud. He speaks alternately with ecstasy and sarcasm, the aspirations of his spirit dragged down by the muddy clay of his physical nature. No unqualified happiness exists here; even in Fairhaven the indulgences of the rich are paid for by the sufferings of the poor. Every happiness is compensated by a greater share of unhappiness, and because happiness consumes itself like a flame, the seed of unhappiness is always sprouting in the midst of happiness. All achievement is futile: the Officer, having been awarded a doctorate, is made to return to grade school again, where he has difficulty remembering the product of two times two.

The worst thing, the Lawyer tells Agnes, is "Repeating everything . . . going through it again!" The successes and pleasures of one day are sour the next. Society, the State, and Fate all conspire to bring down the happy person, and man's lot is to repeat the cycle of success and failure—a dreary round. In despair, Agnes cries, "I won't go back with you. . . . I want to rise to the place I first came from." As a goddess she has that option. But first she wants to know the secret of what lies behind a mysterious door with a clover-shaped keyhole which the Officer has been trying to open since the beginning of the play.

The scene changes to Fingal's cave, where Agnes is talking with the Poet. She sings of human sorrow in a prayer to Indra. They are interrupted by the sight of a ship in distress. Christ appears, walking on the water, to save the sailors, but terrified they jump overboard to their deaths.

Finally a group of experts is assembled to open the mysterious door—the President of a University, Deans of Theology, Philosophy, Medicine, and Law. Bickering incessantly, these pedants finally get the door open—but there is nothing there.

The last scene is outside the castle again. Various characters gather around a fire, sacrificing upon it the emblems of their failure in life. The Daughter of Indra, having experienced the sorrows of the earth even more keenly than mortals can, ascends into the heavens once again, promising to take the complaints of man to the highest throne. The final stage directions, no doubt difficult to execute, read: "The rear of the stage is lit up by the burning castle and reveals a wall of human faces, questioning, sorrowful, despairing. As the castle burns, the flower bud at the top bursts and blossoms into a huge chrysanthemum."[16]

This ending brings a note of peace to the unabated sorrowfulness of the main part of the play. Although the characters, with the exception of the Daughter, do not transcend their suffering, a symbolical transcendence occurs with the flowering of the castle, indicating that the characters have been purified through their tribulations. As the castle has its foundations in the mire, so men are bound down to their bodies; nevertheless they aspire to spiritual goals—peace, bliss, goodness—a tendency reflected in the castle's persistent growth. But each new stage of growth towards higher goals is exposed as an illusion. The maid keeps "pasting and sealing" up the windows as the glazier adds them on. The castle symbolizes, then, the accumulation of man's defeats, and the blossoming of fulfillment comes only when it *burns.*

The burning recalls a passage from the *Bhagavad-Gita:* "He whose every undertaking is free from desire and the incentive thereof, whose action is burnt up in the fire of knowledge, him the knowers of Reality call wise."[17] Described here is the behavior of an enlightened man, who is not attached to his actions, either to their performance or their fruits. He is not bound by the relative world, though he continues to function in it. The characters at the end of *A Dream Play* are in the process of sacrificing their attachments on the fires of knowledge. Here destruction has a positive end, for it is only ignorance that is dying.

The purpose of the play is not to depress us about the sad state of mankind, but to give us a sense of the dreamlike fabric of ordinary life and a vision of the greater reality beyond it. Characters such as the Officer may not be able to have that vision, but the audience can. Strindberg's art is intended to enlighten, not delude (like the illusionist stage). He uses the theatre to dispel illusion; ironically, in the play, the theatre symbolizes the illusions men strive after. The Officer's preoccupation with what is behind that curious door by the theatre, for instance, is a case of the vain search for "meaning" that modern man indulges in.

Why is there nothing beyond that door with its clover-shaped keyhole, seemingly emblematic of good luck? Perhaps because the emptiness that greets the learned Deans is the exact value of their knowledge.

They have mastered the arts of the relative world, which is only a field of emptiness when the greater reality is known. Only that which is unchanging can have lasting value. To look at it from another angle, the nothingness beyond the door is the form in which the ignorant mind conceives transcendence. The transcendent is attributeless; it is devoid of qualities, being infinite and unbounded, therefore incapable of qualification. Unless it is an experiential reality, it can only be conceived from the point of view of what it is not. But this non-concreteness is puzzling to minds attempting to know it only intellectually.

The panic of the sailors who throw themselves overboard when they actually see Christ, to whom they had prayed, walking on the water, is another example of the inadequacy of ordinary minds to comprehend the Absolute. Here the response is fear instead of puzzlement. Strindberg's trenchant implication is that most people who practice religion are actually afraid of encountering the divine. They fear going mad like Pip in the midst of the ocean of the Infinite. Thus the sailors, rather than face the object of their desires, which their awareness is too small to contain, commit suicide. Man's self-destructive tendencies are merely reluctance to wake from the waking dream of ignorance.

Certainly this is also Dostoevsky's point in "The Grand Inquisitor" chapter of *The Brothers Karamazov*. Christ returns to earth and is promptly imprisoned by the Grand Inquisitor, who tells him it would have been better if he had not come back, done miracles, and given people a vision of love, perfection, and righteousness which they couldn't live up to of their own free will. If he must come back, he should set up some sort of fascist theocracy, dispense bread and wine, and force people to be righteous. To live the Ideal is too terrible a charge to lay upon most men, and they must crucify whoever tries to do it.

Typically it is the hero who bursts the boundaries which imprison the masses. The Daughter of Indra is the heroine here. She follows the archetypal pattern of Separation, Initiation, and Return, leaving her home in the heavens for the earthly life, and after being dragged down by it and almost forgetting her divine nature, finally returning. Her pattern is on the same order of Thel's in Blake's *Book of Thel,* except that Thel shied away from leaving the land of Innocence for the cruel world of Experience. There comes a point in every man's evolution where he must leave the comfortable status quo, grapple with the unknown, and hope to win out and grow from the experience. The

Daughter indeed accepts the challenge to descend into matter, and finally she surpasses her entanglement with it. By implication, all men and women are sons and daughters of Indra; her transcendence is an inspiration for all humanity. This may not have been Strindberg's conscious intention, but it is a universal property of all hero stories to reveal the heroic possiblities latent in everybody. All the characters have a bit of the Daughter in them, which accounts for their sympathetic response to her.

In fact, as Strindberg explains it himself, there is but one real character in this drama:

> The characters split, double, multiply, dissolve, condense, float apart, coalesce. But one mind stands over and above them all, the mind of the dreamer; and for him there are no secrets, no inconsistencies, no laws. He does not condemn, does not acquit; he only narrates the story.[18]

Who is the dreamer? All of the characters are aspects of him/her, "an invisible bisexual psyche projecting its extended experience of life through a number of dramatis personae, who form a composite picture of Man and Woman."[19] The Dreamer's point of view is transcendent, like the Author's in *Six Characters,* like Godot's. It is only by assuming that vantage point that we can recognize the action of the play as representative of an illusory state. Strindberg says that at the end the dreamer wakes and embraces Reality, which may be agonizing itself but is in any case preferable to the inferior state of the dream. Evidently he had no great hopes for finding bliss in the Beyond, but he knew the need for transcendence.

Strindberg was subject to rather violent psychological upheavals, so it is no wonder that his work is tainted for many by that personal suffering. But the limitations of Strindberg's consciousness—whatever they were, which is something we don't really know—need not affect our appreciation of his work. *A Dream Play* can uplift and inspire. Strindberg himself alternated between periods of creative depression and fits of inspiration. He was a polymath and wrote voluminously, and he was also mentally unbalanced and relatively inactive for years. A contradictory man, his plays are also full of unresolved oppositions. But by the force of his art he allows his audience to assume the transcendent perspective which he does not explicitly provide.

One of the contradictions will be pointed out by those who see in the Daughter more a temptress than a savior or heroine. In his earlier plays, Strindberg's famous misogyny came out in his depictions of men as victims of demonic women. The case against the Daughter may be summarized in the form of a parable she tells the Poet:

> At the dawn of time before the sun shone, Brahma, the divine primal potency, went forth and let himself be seduced by Maya, the creative mother of the world, in order that he might propagate himself. The divine element thus joined with earthly matter. This was the fall of heaven. Consequently, the world and its inhabitants are nothing more than phantoms, mirages, images in a dream . . .[20]

The Female, then, is responsible, in this somewhat idiosyncratic version of the myth, for the creation of the world of suffering. The Daughter must share this guilt, and her sinking into the mire of earthly existence and tempting the Lawyer to do the same are indicative of her identification with the "evil" earthly element.

Strindberg was very opposed to the feminist impulse of Ibsen's *A Doll's House*. He saw Nora's independence in leaving her unworthy husband as escapist and delusory. He reveals this in *A Dream Play* when the Daughter leaves her marriage with the Lawyer for a trip to Fairhaven with the Officer. Her romantic illusions are satirized: she didn't know that being poor meant having to live in dirt.

Archetypally the female is associated with the earth, the male with the heavens. The powerful ascetic impulse in *A Dream Play* against the snares of the sensory world is by association anti-female. However, I do not feel that the play has a misogynistic tone. Man and woman are equally stuck in the mire of the waking state of consciousness, and he is as guilty for that condition as she is, if guilt must be assigned. If the Officer, for instance, is brought down by his admiration for the inaccessible Miss Victoria, he is at least as culpable as she for his preoccupation. He welcomes being miserable for the sake of yearning after her beauty.

In contrast to Strindberg's asceticism, there is a strong attraction to the world of the senses in the play. The dream landscape is alternately beautiful and horrible; probably a good production should exploit these oppositions to the fullest. Strindberg sees asceticism as futile because it contradicts the natural desire to indulge and fulfill the senses. Even the gods are susceptible to the charms of matter. We shall see in later chapters how the tension between the material and the spiritual, unresolved in this play, can be resolved on the level of consciousness.

Strindberg saw the contradiction as follows, in his diary on the day *A Dream Play* was finished:

> The world has come into existence only through Sin—if in fact it exists at all—for it is really only a dream picture (consequently my *Dream Play* is a picture of life), a phantom, and the ascetic's allotted task is to destroy it. But this task conflicts with the love impulse, and the sum total of it all is a ceaseless wavering between sensual orgies and the anguish of repentance.
>
> This would seem to be the key to the riddle of the world.[21]

The interplay of these opposed tendencies works well for Strindberg as a theatrical device. By representing reality as a dream he allows the audience to gain a separateness from it, an aesthetic distance that he strived for. At the same time we are drawn into the play by empathy with the characters' emotions. This alternation between aesthetic distance and empathy creates in us a habit of mind which may linger after we leave the theatre of feeling apart from and yet a part of the world.

In his occasional revulsion with the "sensual orgies" inherent in the state of waking ignorance, where experience of sensory phenomena predominates over knowledge of the Self, Strindberg is not life-denying. He prophesies a higher life, even though its outlines elude him.

A Dream Play recalls the terrifying images of the wasteland of modern life by another Scandinavian expressionist, Edvard Munch. Both he and Strindberg give more than a glimpse of the skull beneath the skin. Strindberg's vision is more uncompromising than Beckett's or Pirandello's; the only humor that mitigates suffering is for him very black indeed. Yet Strindberg's reminder of the insufficiencies of relative existence gives us more impetus to evolve to higher states. His play dematerializes the relative, transports us from the sphere of naturalistic reality, and kindles the higher life within us. As a work of art it takes us beyond the dualities of beauty and ugliness, wealth and poverty, knowledge and ignorance, pleasure and pain. Life is in flux between these poles, but there need be no suffering on account of that instability, not when through the insubstantial flux we discern the possibility for transcendence.

The sense of a single Dreamer beneath the melange of characters and phantasmagoric images saves the play from chaos. The events do not unfold according to the usual cause-effect exposition, but they possess an associational logic and an underlying controlling intelligence. The unity is so subtle it is as if the play were set in the consciousness of each person who watches it. The characters are abstract and universalized enough that they could be anybody's inner voices. As we watch the play, we look within.

If there is a message to *A Dream Play,* it is this: if we see life as a vale of tears, we see a reflection of our inner state, and we can change the world by changing ourselves. The nightmarish wasteland will vanish when we awaken from our dream.

Strindberg questioned whether the world existed at all. The answer is that it exists insofar as we exist. In the waking state, one's Self is overshadowed and subjective being is minimal. To really *be,* we must consciously realize the pure existence of Self, transcendental consciousness. Only when we are established in the infinitude of pure existence will the world of objects be seen as it is, in its ideal and not merely its transitory surface aspect. Only after we become real (in cosmic consciousness) does the world becomes real (in God consciousness). Finally, in Unity consciousness, we and our environment are in total harmony. The Self encompasses the dream play of the world and awakens it to its fundamental reality as consciousness.

Chapter 3

TRANSCENDENCE

Ingmar Bergman: *The Seventh Seal*
C. G. Jung: *Memories, Dreams, Reflections*
Thomas Pynchon: *The Crying of Lot 49*

The fourth state of consciousness is qualitatively different from the first three states: sleeping, dreaming, and waking. It transcends them because it is non-relative and unchanging. It is beyond thought and yet the very source of thought: the ocean of energy and intelligence from which all thought impulses arise as waves. When, in meditation, awareness settles to a state of least excitation so that all thoughts are stilled, consciousness itself persists. This is transcendental consciousness, consciousness without an object, consciousness in a state not of activity but of pure potentiality.

Transcendental consciousness is synonymous with the big "S" Self: undivided, therefore truly *individual*. A sequence of verses from the *Bhagavad-Gita* explains the nature of the Self:

> He is never born, nor does he ever die; nor once having been, does he cease to be. Unborn, eternal, everlasting, ancient, he is not slain when the body is slain...
>
> Weapons cannot cleave him, nor fire burn him; water cannot wet him, nor wind dry him away.
>
> He is uncleavable; he cannot be burned; he cannot be wetted, nor yet can he be dried. He is eternal, all-pervading, stable, immovable, ever the same.
>
> He is declared to be unmanifest, unthinkable, unchangeable; therefore knowing him as such you should not grieve.[1]

Most of the terms we can find to describe the Self say what it is not— not finite, and so on—for what concept can delineate the illimitable? "Bliss" is one positive term that is often used. At best through words we can only point in the direction of the Absolute, for no words are spoken in that silence.

The mind is naturally attracted within to experience the fullness of its own essential nature in the energy and intelligence that motivate and direct thoughts. All quests, all searches for fulfillment must inevitably point to the goal of transcendental consciousness, the source of life and thought whose nature is bliss.

It might seem incongruous to begin our discussion of bliss consciousness with such a work as Ingmar Bergman's film *The Seventh Seal* (1956). It is dominated in most people's memories by the disquieting figure of Death, who broods omnipresently over the bleak landscape of plague-stricken medieval Europe, ever lurking in the background with his ironic smile. But Death, as a black-robed harbinger of doom with a pasty complexion and an inscrutable expression, is but a projection upon the Unknown of the fears of those in ignorance. For them, in fact, Death is a mirror image of life as they conceive it—a wasteland, a world of emptiness, disease, and despair.

In various forms, death pervades the film. Organized religion seems to serve the Lord of Death: when Antonius Block, a knight returning to his ravaged homeland from the Crusades, goes to confession, Death is the priest in the confessional. Death is found in the robes of the chief monk in charge of torturing and burning to death a young girl accused of being a witch. A procession of penitents stagger through the countryside, flogging themselves to appease the wrathful God who seems to have decided to end the world. And the face of Christ on the church walls is another version of death: full of unmitigated suffering, it is a sign that man has dragged the image of God to the lowest level. The Savior cannot save even himself.

In contrast with these horrors, however, Bergman juxtaposes many images of light which betoken transcendence. The family of actors—Jof, Mia, and their baby—are usually found in light, meadowy surroundings redolent of fertility and happiness. The innocent love shared by the family is a tenuous foil to the gloomy lurking Death who tries to ensnare them. But they turn out to be stronger, with the help of Antonius Block.

True to medieval tradition, the knight Block serves as defender of the Holy Family; for Jof and Mia are like Joseph and Mary in that they unconsciously perpetuate the living spirit of religion. Whereas the Church has abandoned any attempt to foster spiritual growth, Jof and

Mia spontaneously live spiritually healthy lives. They have given birth to a child who symbolizes the eternal creative potential that defies the world of death; they care about each other; they share their wild strawberries with the knight; and Jof has access to a plane of vision that no others do. He can see the Virgin Mary. And he has dreams of teaching his son to do the impossible trick: to juggle the balls and make one of them stand still in the air. As players in a theatrical troupe, Jof and Mia dare to attempt the impossible and transmute the suffering they see around them into comedy through their art. Thus in many ways they represent the resurgence of new life that is the surest emblem of spiritual vitality.

Throughout the film, Block and Death are engaged in a chess game, the knight hoping to outwit the other and save his life. He learns that because Jof and Mia have been traveling with him, their lives will also be forfeited if he loses. Death gains the advantage by playing a trick: in the guise of a priest at confession, he gets the knight to reveal his strategy. Block, in return, "accidentally" knocks over the pieces at a critical point, gaining time for Jof and Mia to escape as Death is preoccupied with setting up the board again.

The confrontation between the knight and Death is that of the heroic man who asks questions, upholds the good, and challenges the darkness in the face of all odds, versus the spirit of entropy and destruction in the universe. Block is not an innocent like Jof and Mia; he has lost his freshness and his idealism in the Crusades. Still it is inconceivable to him to give in to the seemingly irresistible power of Death. To admit the darkness into one's soul is to become like Raval, a theologian who formerly exhorted Block to participate in the Crusades but who now has become a killer and a thief. The struggle is not futile: the soul as well as the body is at stake.

The knight is in the tragic situation of playing a game he cannot win. His loss at chess and his death are inevitable. Still he struggles heroically against the limitations of existence, trying to break its boundaries. His squire Jöns, on the other hand, in the archetypal role of comic sidekick, accepts the world as he finds it and tries to make the best of it. In contrast to his gloomy master, he is jovial; to offset the knight's otherworldly air, he is thoroughly grounded in life's practicalities. Block is plagued with existential doubts; he speculates on whether anything exists beyond this life. He yearns to believe in God and the immortality of the soul but has no experience to support that belief. Jöns is cynically sure that there is only emptiness on the other side of life, a view that Death seems to share when Block asks him what he knows of the other side:

> *Knight:* And you will divulge your secrets.
> *Death:* I have no secrets.
> *Knight:* So you know nothing.
> *Death:* I have nothing to tell.[2]

When Death finally arrives for knight and squire, Jöns clings to his appreciation of the present moment: "In any case, feel the immense triumph of this last minute when you can still roll your eyes and move your toes." But Block's thoughts are wholly on the future: "God, You who are somewhere, who *must* be somewhere, have mercy upon us."[3] Neither one is wrong. Life is a dialectical progression of tragedy and comedy. Comedy revels in the moment, accepts boundaries and limitations and imperfect human nature, but tragedy forges into the future, bucks the odds and Fate, and tries to dissolve all encroachments on freedom. Without comedy there is no form and no stability; without tragedy, no evolution.

Block's point of view is more dominant because this work is a tragedy, and its purpose is to affirm the possibilities for transcendence in a world where the limitations have clearly become intolerable. The tragic hero sacrifices himself for the sake of a greater life: the self dies and the Self is born. The tragic catharsis is the relief an audience feels in sharing the hero's experience of relieving himself of the cares that have compressed his consciousness into a narrow sphere. When King Lear divests himself of his "lendings," he is stripping off the constraints of his superficial identity and uncovering the potential of his greater consciousness. The loss implicit in tragedy is a loss of ignorance, and an effective tragedy will show there is cause for joy behind the tears. An empty, meaningless death is neither tragic nor heroic. The purpose of tragedy is to demonstrate the greater wholeness of which death is only a part.

When Death takes the knight and his friends at the end of the play, Jof sees them with the eye of vision in "a solemn dance toward the dark lands, while the rain washes their faces and cleans the salt of the tears from their cheeks."[4] The image of Death, which has been so malevolent throughout, reflecting the evil and disease that rage in the world of the living, becomes almost benevolent. He is a purgative power that releases men from their spiritual sickness and delivers them into a new life. That renewed life is already being enjoyed by Jof and Mia and their son, who wander off together happily at the end in a scene uncommonly filled with sunlight.

The image of the Dance of Death conveys an orderliness and harmony that signals a rejuvenation for the chaotic society. This awesome, moving, profoundly peaceful scene contrasts with the Dance of Death painted on the wall of a church earlier in the film, which renders Death only in its horrific aspect. The reality turns out to be an improvement on the painter's vision, which reflects the superficial level of death. Walt Whitman's assertion in "Song of Myself" comes to mind:

> All goes onward and outward, nothing collapses,
> And to die is different from what any supposed, and
>   luckier.[5]

Archetypically, death is a metaphor for immersion in transcendental consciousness, the source and goal of life. St. Paul said, "I die daily," meaning that he regularly experienced this replenishment of consciousness. Dying is dyeing. As a cloth gets colored by repeated dippings, so the mind gets infused with the nature of pure consciousness through repeated exposure and becomes permanently saturated with intelligence, creativity, and clarity.

The character's differing views of Death reestablish the principle that knowledge is structured in consciousness. Those in deepest ignorance perceive Death as a finality and an emptiness, a great unknown to be feared. To the common people, the idea of trying to contest with Death is inconceivable. The knight has the imagination to challenge Death to a chess game, though he knows that at best he is only buying time against the inevitable. He is not afraid and refuses to accept that Death means ultimate emptiness. He feels strongly there must be something beyond life, but assurances from the Church are no consolation. He must know it first-hand. This passion for direct spiritual experience enlivens his consciousness and structures a different aspect of Death for him than for most. Death is an equal rather than a master, and the end result of death does, indeed, turn out luckier than supposed.

Birgitta Steene, in her commentary on *The Seventh Seal,* has said that the knight's passion for knowledge of God, for direct revelation, is the same as Adam and Eve's original sin of desire for ultimate knowledge.[6] But surely it is a misconception that the fall of man was

41

brought about because of his desire to know God. Human life can only fall from bliss to suffering if it is not established in transcendental consciousness. Dulled intelligence leads to wrong decisions resulting in bad repercussions. The original sin was in not desiring *enough* knowledge; that is, in being satisfied with knowledge of the relative and not hungering after the Absolute. The desire to know more is the very impulse of life: such a good becomes evil only if it manifests partially. In the film, the knight is not chastened for his extraordinary passion: rather, he and his friends enjoy a special grace at the end as a result of his courageous and energetic questing for truth.

The note of hope that ends the film is all the stronger in contrast to the bleakness of the medieval wasteland that has been painted throughout. In prophesying a way out for both knight and Holy Family—representing the intellectual and the emotional sides of the human being—Bergman goes beyond the explorations of Strindberg, one of his mentors. In *The Seventh Seal,* as in *A Dream Play,* life is presented as a duel of opposites: life and death, organized religion and true spirituality, asceticism and pleasure, tragedy and comedy. The dramatic light and dark imagery punctuates the theme: life as a battleground of ignorant armies. But whereas in Strindberg nothing in the relative has a stable value, in Bergman's world we are made to feel intimations of immortality. The knight's heroism, the family's innocent love and perpetuation of artistic values, the earthy vitality of the commoners—these are the manifestations of the continuity of consciousness that underlies changing life. Bergman's characters are more substantial than Strindberg's, and they are more joyous, able to see glimpses of immanent Being penetrating the wasteland of the senses. Wild strawberries and milk are the visible, tangible signs of God's grace to the knight, who up until the picnic with Jof and Mia has been tormented by doubts of his faith. He says:

> I shall remember this moment. The silence, the twilight, the bowls of strawberries and milk, your faces in the evening light. Mikael sleeping, Jof with his lyre. I'll try to remember what we talked about. I'll carry this memory between my hands as carefully as if it were a bowl filled to the brim with fresh milk. (He turns his face away and looks out toward the sea and the colorless gray sky) And it will be an adequate sign—it will be enough for me.[7]

The simple things in life are the most eternal, and this transcendent moment of peace, apart form the madness, bolsters him for the resumption of his chess game with Death. Thus Bergman emphasizes the Oneness that upholds the multiplicity and oppositions of life.

The title of the film comes from the Book of Revelation, in which the Lamb of God breaks seven seals on the Book of God, which contains the supreme revelation. For every seal that is opened, some catastrophe strikes: the Four Horsemen of the Apocalypse come out to wreak havoc, there is a great earthquake, and the sun becomes as black as sackcloth of hair. When the seventh seal is opened, "there was silence in heaven about the space of half an hour." Then after some angelic announcements accompanied by various cataclysms, Christ descends to establish God's kingdom on earth.

D. H. Lawrence in his commentary on Revelation, *Apocalypse,* interprets the recondite symbolism in terms of an event in the life of every individual, instead of a cosmic event, the end of the world. He sees the apocalypse as an immanent rather than an imminent happening: everyone has the present potential to destroy ignorance and gain enlightenment, and whether the world itself is destroyed some time in the future is less important. As for the seven seals, he says:

> The famous book of seven seals in this place is the body of man: of a man: of Adam: of any man: and the seven seals are the seven centres or gates of his dynamic consciousness. We are witnessing the opening and conquest of the great psychic centers of the human body. The old Adam is going to be conquered, die, and be reborn as the new Adam: but in stages: in six stages, and then a climax, seven.[8]

The "Living I" is the seventh and subtlest of man's physical and spiritual natures that are stripped away as the seals are opened. Each opening is accompanied by symbolism of destruction because each is a stage of "mystic death." What remains when the first six levels of individuality have been systematically transcended is "my very me, my sacred ego, called into a new cycle of action by the Lamb and riding forth to conquest, the conquest of the old self for the birth of a new self."[9] In other words, the Book of Revelation is a description of an initiatory rite in which the initiate is brought to the experience of the absolute, unbounded essential Self. This is a death and a rebirth because it is an end to bondage to the relative and a beginning of awareness of the transcendent inner Being.

Bergman's Biblical allusions can best be understood as reflecting a universal process of individual evolution. Just as the Initiation phase of the monomyth can be seen as analogous to transcendental consciousness, as I mentioned in Chapter One, so here the knight, who undergoes death, and, we are given to understand, a rebirth, is Everyman in the process of discovering the "Living I," the bliss of the Absolute.

The reason he finally accepts death is that he has discovered, through the dialectic of his game with the black-hooded figure, the complementarity of life and death that is reflected in his travels from the joyous family circle of Jof and Mia to the hideous, plague-ridden corpse-strewn landscapes. The creative and destructive processes of life go together. The nature of relative life is change, and without destruction nothing new can come into being. Underneath the changes is an eternal current which promises that though there may be death, there is no extinction—only greater and greater fulfillment and consciousness. So Antonius Block joins the ordered measure of Death's dance, to become aware of that universal ocean on whose surface he has been only a wave, like the meditator whose mind settles down from the excitement of thoughts and perceptions to a profound inner silence.

C. G. Jung is included in this primarily literary study because he was devoted to uncovering the transcendent Self, both in his own life and in the lives of his patients, and also through a wide range of anthropological, religious, philosophical, and literary studies. Freud peered into these traditions as well, but he dismissed the notion of transcendental consciousness in *Civilization and its Discontents* as a kind of infantile regression. Though Freud may have had more influence than Jung on the shaping of modern psychological theory, it is likely that Jung's pioneering researches will be vindicated with the current explosion of people having and acknowledging transcendental experiences. Jung's inclusion here is additionally relevant for his influence in the development of archetypal criticism and mythological study.

Jung believed that the unconscious is at the deepest level *collective*: the repository of all the archetypes that manifest in human myth, art, dreams, and waking behavior patterns. The most fundamental of these archetypes is that of the Self, the sum of the conscious and unconscious mind, and at the same time the center of one's total being. Jung says that the God-image is the projection of that archetype; thus when we worship God we are revering our own deepest being.

Humanity has represented the Self in many forms. Jung wrote of the mythos of the Anthropos, or gigantic cosmic man, the original ancestor of the human race, its collective soul, as a symbol of the inner man. He found the Anthropos in the Mercurius of the medieval alchemists, in the sacred phallus of the Ophite Gnostics, in the Indian Purusha, in the Norse Ymir, in the Chinese P'an Ku, in the Merlin of the Grail legends. And in *Memories, Dreams, Reflections* (1961), he tells of finding the Anthropos in his own life, in an aspect of himself that he called the "No. 2" personality.

As a schoolboy, Jung first became aware of this other self in a flash of insight:

> I was taking the long road to school . . . when suddenly for a single moment I had the overwhelming impression of having just emerged from a dense cloud. I knew all at once: now I am myself! . . . Previously I had existed, too, but everything had merely happened to me. Now I happened to myself. Now I knew: I am myself now, now I exist.[10]

The schoolboy of 1890 was the No. 1 self, but Jung felt the essential self, the No. 2, to be an old man living in the eighteenth century with buckled shoes and a white wig. He carried a consciousness of this imposing other self throughout his childhood, and it endowed him with a sense of authority and stability. He could pass over into a state of identification with No. 2 whenever alone, and at such times he felt, "Here nothing separated man from God; indeed, it was as though the human mind looked down upon creation simultaneously with God."[11]

As a child Jung consoled himself in times of stress by sitting on a large stone in his garden and imagining that he was the stone:

> Whenever I thought that I was the stone, the conflict ceased. "The stone has no uncertainties, no urge to communicate, and is eternally the same for thousands of years," I would think, "while I am only a passing phenomenon which bursts into all kinds of emotions, like a

flame that flares up quickly and then goes out." I was but the sum of my emotions, and the Other in me was the timeless, imperishable stone.[12]

This early identification of the stone with the No. 2 self was later extended in his alchemical studies when he identified the philosopher's stone as a symbol of the immortal Christ body of every man, the immanence of spirit fixed in matter. The stone was the means by which an alchemist could transmute matter into spirit and identify himself with the Anthropos of his discipline, Mercurius, the transcendent world-soul. Stone also became important to Jung later in life when he felt the urge to construct model villages in stone by his lakeside house at Küsnacht. After that he built a house for himself out of stone at Bollingen, which gave him "a feeling as if I were being reborn in stone. It is thus a concretization of the individuation process . . ."[13]

"Individuation" was Jung's term for the process of becoming a whole, indivisible person. He saw human life as progressing towards unity, a unity with the higher Self. An individuated person would have an awareness of the Self and would have integrated the Self with the ego, the center of the conscious mind. Most people seemed cut off from their essential Being; it was buried in their unconscious. They confused the ego (or small self) with the big Self and thus restricted their chance to grow, to become true individuals by expanding the ego to universal Self.

We could cite many of Jung's personal experiences as evidence for the growing awareness of Self in his own life. One time when he was near death in a hospital, he felt himself high in space, looking down upon the earth, which was radiating a beautiful blue light. All the details were clear. During another vision he had the sensation of having "the whole phantasmagoria of earthly existence" stripped away, down to some irreducible identity that was the sum of all he had ever been or done, "a feeling of extreme poverty, but at the same time of great fullness."[14] Or he would lie in an ecstasy:

> I felt as though I were floating in space, as though I were safe in the womb of the universe—in a tremendous void, but filled with the highest possible feeling of happiness. "This is eternal bliss," I thought. "This cannot be described; it is far too wonderful."[15]

These clear experiences of transcendental consciousness, sometimes coupled with other sensations and perceptions of a gloriously refined nature, had a quality of "absolute objectivity." Jung felt he was in "Eternity," which he defined as "the ecstasy of a non-temporal state in which present, past, and future are one. . . . Nothing was distributed over time, nothing could be measured by temporal concepts."[16]

Jung's life was characterized from beginning to end by frequent encounters with transcendence, and his experience of the deepest levels of the psyche profoundly influenced his psychological studies. From Jung's point of view, Freud looked at man too much in terms of what was unhealthy rather than what was healthy, and misplaced the role of sexuality in the psychic life. Jung saw sexuality as an expression of the unconscious divine energy in man, but Freud made a god of the sexual libido in its bodily aspect. Thus for Freud reality was physical and limited, whereas Jung tended to look beyond the repressed drives and feelings (such as the desire for incest), to "climb out of the mud of the commonplace": "How are they ever to emerge if analysis does not make them aware of something different or better, when even theory holds them fast in it and offers them nothing more than the rational or 'reasonable' injunction to abandon such childishness?"[17] Not content to deal with problems on their own restricted level, Jung sought the field of bliss consciousness, which was in its fullness of awareness the answer to the more limited human strivings and neuroses connected with the body.

Jung called his life "a story of the self-realization of the unconscious."[18] The unconscious, he said, naturally wants to become conscious; there is a tendency for whatever is buried inside to come out into the clear light. This idea is in accord with Maharishi's insistence that life is in a state of perpetual growth, and that consciousness is accordingly always evolving to higher states by its own nature.

Jung saw a danger to the conscious mind that it could be swallowed up by the unconscious. In dictatorships, for example, people let themselves be robbed of the possibility for transcendence and slip into relative unconsciousness for the sake of the State, which assumes their moral will. There are certain archetypal unconscious forces that Jung thought it necessary to confront in the individuation process and integrate into one's consciousness. The "shadow" is the apparently evil or simply mysterious aspect of the personality which is projected onto other people when not recognized as a force within the psyche. The "anima" is the feminine nature in men, the "animus" the masculine nature in women, and these images can also be projected. If I as a man, for instance, deny the fact that I have any aspect of femininity in my nature, I will confront the image of my anima in women, whom I will perceive as tempting or threatening me. In short, the shadow, the anima, and the animus become dangerous forces when not recognized and assimilated. Because the nature of the unconscious contents is to become conscious, these archetypes force themselves on the outer attention when the inward eye is blinded.

In the individuated person, the masculine and feminine elements are in a state of dynamic equilibrium, as in the black and white circle of the Tao, a symbol of the Self. The archetypal powers are hostile only when not integrated into the conscious personality. The assimilation of these powers leads to a more normal functioning of mind and body and a greater balance between intellect and emotions. Direct experience of the Self spontaneously cultures the growth of integration throughout the personality, including its subtle, transpersonal component.

This component, Jung's "collective unconscious," is the repository of all manner of archetypal images, benevolent or malevolent, wise men, gods, kings, and also demons, witches, and ghosts. Attacking the ambiguous nature of Jung's concept of the unconscious, Titus Burkhardt, in an essay entitled "Cosmology and Modern Science," has accused Jung of spiritual dilettantism, of confusing influences from the "inferior psychism," such as lower, animal drives or even psychic influences coming from unknown entities, with the transcendent higher Self. He criticizes Jung for failing to distinguish Inferno from Paradiso in the realm of the unconscious, and for regarding the impulses of the collective unconscious as a result of biological determinism—an inherited, automatic set of responses, something on the level of animal instinct.[19]

Part of the problem may lie with Jung's use of the term "unconscious." Certainly transcendental consciousness is unconscious to a person who does not know how to experience it. The Self is like an Other to him. But ultimately transcendental consciousness is the source of whatever awareness the conscious mind possesses, and when the mind settles down in meditation and becomes aware of its source, the unconscious becomes conscious. Thus it is misleading to use the term "unconscious" to include the Self, as if unconsciousness were its ultimate nature. Only from a certain relative standpoint is transcendental consciousness unconscious.

There is in the unconscious a great deal of the "inferior psychism," of which it is questionable that we should want to be conscious. This applies to the collective as well as the personal unconscious. Jung's attitude seems to be that we should recognize unconscious contents regardless of whether they are positive or negative. In Jung's idea of the unconscious we have both the absolute component of the Self along with what we might call, for want of a better term, all the garbage. In this book I have been following Maharishi's lead and considering the conscious thinking mind as only a part of consciousness, with the ultimate, all-inclusive level of consciousness existing at the very source of all thought. Jung's concept of consciousness as pertaining only to the sphere of the conscious mind is too small. It is certainly the conventional use of the word, but it is outmoded in a time when many are experiencing that pure consciousness of which the conscious mind is only a surface layer. And that pure consciousness has become enlivened because imperceptibly, during meditation, someone has come and taken the garbage out.

It is to Jung's credit that he recognized the danger of succumbing to the unprogressive tendencies of the unconscious. He proved resistant in his travels in Africa, for instance, to "going native," or allowing the primitive forces of his unconscious to overcome him (à la "Mistah Kurtz"). His spirit inclined towards an active confrontation rather than a passive acceptance of such forces.

His goal in life was indeed to carry the light of the conscious mind into the dark reaches, not to let that light be extinguished but to make it brighter. Jung's *Memories, Dreams, Reflections*, Laurens van der Post's *Jung and the Story of Our Time*, and Marie-Louise von Franz's *C. G. Jung: His Myth in Our Time* convincingly show the overall integrity, wholeness, and balance of Jung's life and thought, and by comparison make Burkhardt's critique seem peevish, as if he were determined to see the thorn at the expense of the rose.

Jung brought, into a dichotomized culture, the concept of the Self as a principle of balance between opposites. The transcendent is a field of supreme orderliness against which the relatedness of relative adversaries becomes clear. Take, for instance, science and religion. Jung attempted to study the mind objectively and scientifically, and yet his conclusions were metaphysical. He traced the causes of pathological behavior to a lack of awareness of the transcendental Self, beyond all conditioned and conscious control. The domain of the Self had traditionally been a religious concern, not considered relevant by science because it could not be measured.

When science and religion extend themselves to the most profound level, however, they reach a point of intersection. A religion serious about developing the inner man in order to uplift him morally and spiritually must find a scientifically verifiable technique to accomplish that in order that its results be real and repeatable, not imagined. And science, in studying the relative phenomenal world and its laws, must inevitably be drawn to the home of those laws in the Absolute, which is consciousness itself and the goal of the religious quest. Thus science and religion are partners in man's evolution to higher states of consciousness. The conflicts are illusory.

Jung helped to bridge the appalling abyss between the two, and as Laurens van der Post notes, his therapeutic work was not separable from the religious function:

> Healing the sick without a requickening of religion, as he put it to me, was "just not on." He was back at the moment far back in time when the world "heal" formed itself first on the lips of living men, and to heal meant to "make whole," and wholly and holy were both derived from "heal" to describe an indivisible concept of life, so that in the beginning, as in this hour so much later than we think, the condition of wholeness and that of holiness are synonymous. This was the condition symbolised by the finding of the Holy Grail, the transcendental vessel— "graille" was an old Provencal word for a vessel— wherein the spirit in all its apparent self contradictions could be poured and contained as at one and whole.[20]

Jung's concern with total healing—that is, with finding transcendental wholeness—led him to researches in myth and religion which voluminously substantiate the universality of the archetype of the Self. In the process he discovered that the medieval science of alchemy was first and foremost a science of consciousness, with a symbology whose literal level of the transmutation of lead into gold had a more subtle meaning in the transfiguration of the limited egoistic human into the divine-human cosmic creative body of Mercurius, the Anthropos.

Jung's syncretic studies have helped to bridge Eastern and Western thought as well as science and religion. In his commentaries on the *I*

Ching and *The Secret of the Golden Flower* he related such Chinese concepts of the Self as the Tao and the "diamond body" to the Pauline Christ symbol. He showed that though the East and West were poles apart in their symbolism they were together in their goal. Jung did not have as profound an understanding of Indian religion, however. He saw the goal of Indian meditation as mere "emptiness," as opposed to his own goal of unfolding Being in terms of concrete, natural life. He was apparently not informed about the positive aspect of the Vedic conception of the Absolute and the possibility of higher states such as God consciousness and Unity consciousness, in which the transcendental Self is realized along with perception of nature's fullness. Otherwise he probably would not have found a difference between Indian ideals and his own.

Another abyss Jung has helped to bridge is the radical dualism in Western thought between man and God, and at no time has this been more acute than in the twentieth century. The advancements of Renaissance science called into question the popular concepts of the Chain of Being and the geocentric universe, which had at least a psychological validity in enabling man to find a link with God and a place for himself in the vast natural order. Unfortunately in a secularized world there was nothing to fill man's need for relatedness to the Absolute; thus the main intellectual trend in this century has been the search for meaning in life.

Jung said he preferred the term "unconscious" to "God" for the inner *nous,* for it seemed better adapted to scientific terminology and did not personify or confer an emotional quality on that transcendent dimension of the Self. What difference is there ultimately, then, between God and man? To Jung, if man is enlightened then God is alive in him:

> Only then can he become whole and only then can "God be born," that is, enter into human reality and associate with man in the form of "man." By this act of incarnation man—that is, his ego—is inwardly replaced by "God," and God becomes outwardly man, in keeping with the saying of Jesus: "Who sees me, sees the Father."[21]

So when the Self is substituted for the ego as the center of conscious life, man and God are essentially at one. But simply to say that man becomes God is to blur Jung's point. He is close to Maharishi, who has said that God may be considered as having two aspects: the impersonal Absolute which is the field of universality and which excludes nothing; and the personal creative being, the conscious, individualized agency that calls the vast display of relative life into existence.[22] Transcendental consciousness is the Self of all beings, God and man included, but man and God are still separate entities. Man's glory is to achieve the same universal status from which the creator of the universe operates and to animate his life with the divine energy and intelligence.

Jung has brought back the doctrine of God's immanence in a secular age, but not in such a way as to deny God's transcendence. As creator, God is by definition beyond His creation; but if man has no direct access to God, and on the absolute level a common conscious-ness with God, then God is not omnipresent and that too contradicts definition. To give the doctrine of Christ's divinity a universal appli-cability, Jung interpreted it to signify the immanent presence of God in the soul of every man and God's desire that all men should become Christified—sons of God, fully cognizant of their divine nature. And yet God remains God and man remains man:

> . . . even the enlightened person remains what he is, and is never more than his own limited ego before the One who dwells within him, whose form has no knowable boundaries, who encompasses him on all sides, fathomless as the abysms of the earth and vast as the sky. [23]

It is clear that Jung knew that humanity has a transcendental nature, and he did everything in his power to help people realize it. His influ-ence on our age has been justifiably great.

As Jung used myth to synthesize scientific and religious values, so does that exuberant novelist Thomas Pynchon. The great American myth of the journey westward to the Promised Land has of necessity been transformed into the discovery of new countries of the soul. Pyn-chon sets *The Crying of Lot 49* (1966) on the West Coast, the leading edge of this transformation, in which both science and religion will be seen to play significant roles. The heroine is named Oedipa Maas, and the story is of her quest—ostensibly for the secret of an organization named Tristero, but on a deeper level for some oasis in the wasteland of twentieth century America.

52

Pynchon surveys the contemporary scene in all its hip and trendy diversity, unstinting in his manic laughter towards a menagerie of Southern California types. There is Mucho Maas, Oedipa's husband, a used-car salesman turned disc jockey who gulps LSD and chases teeny-boppers. There is Dr. Hilarius, her Freudian psychiatrist, an ex-Nazi who experimented in concentration camps on inducing insanity by making faces too hideous to behold. There is Metzger, a lawyer and former child-star "Baby Igor" who is fixated on his lost youth and eventually elopes with "a depraved 15-year-old." There is Randolph Driblette, a solipsistic director who commits suicide after his production of an obscure Jacobean tragedy closes. There is Mike Fallopian, a partisan of the right-wing Peter Pinguid Society, opposed to "industrial anything." There is John Nefastis, inventor of a perpetual-motion machine, who enjoys having sex in front of the TV during the evening news. There is Emery Bortz, an English professor who spends his days in a hammock, surrounded by graduate students, drinking beer and pontificating. There are the Paranoids, a teenage rock & roll band, who sport identical bangs and mohair suits and drooping jaws. There is Pierce Inverarity, a dead multimillionaire, who has single-handedly built an empire of shopping centers, tract houses, and industrial complexes in the decadent paradise of San Narciso, California.

Oedipa herself starts as a typical middle American housewife, but soon she gets the "call to adventure"—the first stage of the mon-omythic quest. She is named executor of Pierce Inverarity's will. A former lover of his, she had once traveled to Mexico with him, where a particular painting captured her eye:

> . . . in the central painting of a triptych, titled "Bordando el Manto Terrestre," were a number of frail girls with heart-shaped faces, huge eyes, spun-gold hair, prisoners in the top room of a circular tower, embroidering a kind of tapestry which spilled out the slit windows and into a void: for all the other buildings and creatures, all the waves, ships and forests of the earth were contained in this tapestry, and the tapestry was the world.[24]

She identifies with Rapunzel, trapped in a tower, letting her hair down into a void and hoping someone will climb it.

The thing that comes to her out of the void is Tristero. In her peregrinations she gradually becomes aware that underneath such massive enterprises as Yoyodyne, Pierce's giant aerospace corporation, there lurks an anti-establishment counterforce. It seems that Yoyodyne employees use an alternate mail service called W.A.S.T.E. Alerted by an allusion in *The Courier's Tragedy,* a Jacobean revenge play, she learns of a mysterious organization called Tristero, one of whose chief operations has for centuries been to run a private mail service and to sabotage the established one.

In Oedipa's attempt to execute Pierce's will, "to bestow life on what had persisted," Tristero continues to intrude. As she struggles through the bewildering maze of Pierce's holdings, the cryptic image of a muted post-horn—the sign of Tristero—confronts her again and again, and she feels compelled to find out more about it.

In her quest for Tristero she is the sole adventurer. Her husband Mucho, as well as Metzger, Driblette, and all the other men she meets are but fragmented personalities, and all resort to escapism to protect themselves from the potentially frightening realizations that she is making. But she doubts her own ability to complete the quest:

> Oedipa wondered whether, at the end of this (if it were supposed to end), she too might not be left with only compiled memories of clues, announcements, intimations, but never the central truth itself, which must somehow each time be too bright for her memory to hold: which must always blaze out, destroying its own message irreversibly, leaving an overexposed blank when the ordinary world came back.[25]

How can the finite mind, indeed, grasp and hold the infinite, even if it is able to glimpse it? Oedipa seeks some ultimate wholeness, knowing that to refuse the challenge will strand her in some spiritual desert like the one Mucho inhabits. Saturated with LSD, he cannot distinguish the edges of things, and his individuality is subsumed by pseudomysticism:

> "Whenever I put the headset on now," he'd continued, "I really do understand what I find there. When those kids sing about 'She loves you,' yeah well, you know, she does, she's any number of people, all over the world, back through time, different colors, sizes ages, shapes, distances from death, but she loves. And the 'you' is

everybody. And herself. Oedipa, the human voice, you know, it's a flipping miracle."[26]

Mucho ends his quest in a false absolute. Driblette, the solipsistic director, does the same. He invests all his energies on the play, making it a little universe that he projects, like the dark machine in the center of a planetarium. When the run of the play is over, he cannot sustain the vision of a random world beyond his control, and so he takes a walk "into that vast sink of the primal blood of the Pacific."

Tristero is more than vaguely malevolent. It is represented in *The Courier's Tragedy* by masked figures dressed entirely in black who assassinate an evil duke. After Oedipa traces the text of the play to a used bookstore to procure the only remaining copy, the store mysteriously burns down. Because she is the only person aware of the monolithic extent of the Tristero conspiracy, she wonders at times if she is not just succumbing to paranoia. But there is ample evidence that she, unlike Driblette, is not merely projecting her world.

She finds that the W.A.S.T.E. system is virtually omnipresent, and that all the lost, alienated souls of this chaotic society are using it in an attempt to have real communication with one another. The official channels of the U.S. Mail are not appropriate for their deepest secrets. But W.A.S.T.E. offers them some hope: "Decorating each alienation, each species of withdrawal, as cufflink, decal, aimless doodling, there was somehow always the post horn."[27]

The search for Tristero leads her to the slums, where she comes into touch with a real person, so different from the lunatics she has been associating with. The man is an old sailor suffering from delirium tremens, one of the numberless lost souls, with a post horn tattooed on his hand:

> She was overcome all at once by a need to touch him, as if she could not believe in him, or would not remember him, without it. Exhausted, hardly knowing what she was doing, she came the last three steps and sat, took the man in her arms, actually held him, gazing out of her smudged eyes down the stairs, back into the morning. She felt wetness against her breast and saw that he was crying again. He hardly breathed but tears came as if being pumped. "I can't help," she whispered, rocking him, "I can't help."[28]

But she can. She acts as a mother-goddess, bringing fertility back to the wasteland of modern life, fighting with tenderness the conformity, uniformity, and technological flash created by the likes of Pierce Inverarity and the Protestant-capitalist tradition. That tradition created a mass of have-nots as well as haves, and the have-nots, according to Calvinist theology, are the preterite, those passed-over, the damned. Oedipa rediscovers part of herself among the have-nots.

Oedipa is uncertain by the end of the novel whether Tristero is part of Pierce's empire, whether he had left that too as part of his inheritance. Why did he possess a collection of stamps that included Tristero forgeries of conventional stamps? The issue is left unresolved, but she does realize that her quest to order Pierce's world has led her to the secret of the nation itself: "She had dedicated herself, weeks ago, to making sense of what Inverarity had left behind, never suspecting that the legacy was America."[29]

Thus the real inheritors of the Inverarity empire are the disinherited anonymous masses, the true Americans. Standing on a railroad track, she has an epiphany: she thinks of the kids, squatters, drifters who followed the tracks, sleeping in junkyards and freight cars, sharing a secret language, "as if they were in exile from somewhere else invisible yet congruent with the cheered land she lived in."[30] And Tristero is the secret voice, muted like the post horn, but omnipresent, indomitable.

In the final scene of the novel, Oedipa attends an auction of Pierce's Tristero forgeries, and Loren Passerine, "the finest auctioneer in the West," is "crying" the sale of these stamps:

> The men inside the auction room wore black mohair and had pale, cruel faces. They watched her come in, trying each to conceal his thoughts. Loren Passerine, on his podium, hovered like a puppet-master, his eyes bright, his smile practiced and relentless. He stared at her, smiling, as if saying, I'm surprised you actually came. . . . An assistant closed the heavy door on the lobby windows and the sun. She heard a lock snap shut; the sound echoes a moment. Passerine spread his arms in a gesture that seemed to belong to the priesthood of some remote culture; perhaps to a descending angel. The auctioneer cleared his throat. Oedipa settled back, to await the crying of lot 49.[31]

It is perhaps futile to try to explain this ending, for the sense of ambiguity, of a mystery that is too bright (or too dark) for the mind to hold, is surely part of Pynchon's intention. But two things at least are clear: first, Tristero exists; it is not a product of Oedipa's paranoia. There is a hidden meaning behind the surface appearances of American life. Second, a religious initiation rite of sorts is beginning. Oedipa is about to learn whether Tristero is evil or whether it merely has a forbidding aspect. Certainly it is easy to fear the unknown, and when Tristero's mysteries are revealed to her, it may be that Oedipa will not feel impelled, like Oedipus, to pluck out her eyes.

Pynchon's allusion to Oedipus is purposeful. *Oedipus Rex* is also a detective story, and it ends with the seeker reaching the goal of his quest in himself. Oedipus's determination to find the culprit that was bringing the gods' disfavor upon Thebes resulted in the discovery of his incest and patricide. The play echoes the theme that knowledge is structured in consciousness: that the evil or good we see outside us is a reflection of the quality we harbor within. But Oedipa is a relative innocent, and Pynchon's novel lacks a tragic tone. Her sensitivity enabled her to detect Tristero, and her sympathy with the plight of the disinherited masses of the earth has entitled her to initiation. I am tempted to read the ending of *The Crying of Lot 49* as ultimately hopeful.

Tristero, in its "cruel" aspect, is like the sphinx that posed the riddle to Oedipus, "What walks on four legs in the morning, two legs in the afternoon, and three in the evening?" Oedipus's answer was "Man" (a baby crawls, an adult stands upright, an old man hobbles on a cane). This too is Oedipa's way of answering the riddle of Tristero. Her realization that the spirit of the American people is "coded" in Pierce Inverarity's testament shows that she has penetrated to the *human* level of the riddle.

As a heroine, Oedipa is about to experience the mythic transcendence at the end of the quest. She is no longer the damsel locked in the tower waiting for rescue from without, weaving her tapestry of delusion to pass the time. She has become an agent for order, leaving the insularity of her home, venturing into dangerous, unknown regions, and attempting to bridge the world of appearances with the "transcendent meaning" that Tristero represents.

Oedipa is, in fact, a Maxwell's Demon. This is an imaginary being invented by the physicist James Clerk Maxwell that is an important motif in the novel. As it is explained to Oedipa:

The Demon could sit in a box among air molecules that were moving at all different random speeds, and sort out the fast molecules from the slow ones. Fast molecules have more energy than slow ones. Concentrate enough of them in one place and you have a region of high temperature. You can then use the difference in temperature between this hot region of the box and any cooler region, to drive a heat engine. Since the Demon only sat and sorted, you wouldn't have put any real work into the system. So you would be violating the Second Law of Thermodynamics, getting something for nothing, causing perpetual motion.[32]

Without going into the complexities of the Nefastis machine which operates on this principle, it is possible to compare Oedipa to Maxwell's Demon because she sorts through the various clues she is presented with and comes out with energy in the form of greater information. Not really a have or a have-not, neither in the Establishment nor out of it, she can monitor the border line between the two and attempt to reduce the entropy, or amount of disorderliness or randomness, in the system she perceives. By sorting the hot and cold molecules—that is, the elect and the preterite—she learns of the existence of the alienated people of the world, represented by Tristero. The Second Law of Thermodynamics holds that entropy is inexorably increasing in the universe, but she circumvents that law and creates more orderliness through the information between her sorting Demon and her surface consciousness. To keep this flow going is to defy the Second Law; if the information were not communicated then its greater potential for randomness would cause the Second Law to prevail again.

This Demon is the *daimon*, the intuitive intellect of man which often in Greek tragedy appears as a powerful external force, a god (like Apollo in *Oedipus Rex*) who forces the hero towards an action that may have tragic consequences but is ultimately for the best. Oedipa listens to her Demon and thus has the only chance of anybody in the novel of resisting the entropic drift that is slowly but surely engulfing Mucho, Driblette, Hilarius, Metzger, and the rest, like the tide of "the primal blood of the Pacific."

The surface of phenomenal life is a constant ebb and flow; nothing lasts, especially in a superficial culture like Pynchon's California. To "go with the flow" in that tide is to commit spiritual suicide. The false absolute that Mucho and Driblette sought through sensation dissolved the boundaries of their egos in the infinitely changing field of sense perceptions. The conscious ego, for all its shortcomings, is at least a link with a greater consciousness, and this Oedipa intuits. So she holds on to her individual ego while communing with the Demon that leads her on her quest for Tristero. Only that way can she find the greater wholeness of Self that has its basis in the true Absolute: in non-change rather than in change.

Pynchon challenges us all to wake our Demons and sort through the amazing amount of information he gives us in this short book. The more we read it, the less chaotic it seems. Finally, Pynchon seems as purposeful as Joyce in his integration of every detail, every allusion, every word into a greater overall plan. The communication current of his mind to ours produces zero entropy.

Pynchon seems to be able to embrace all contradictions. He fills his novels with topical allusions to contemporary culture that are at the same time mythic. His incessant satire always has a seriocomic edge. His scientific background is reflected in the fact that he does not give technology a "bad guy" image as much modern fiction does. Indeed, he finds scientific language rich in metaphors to describe the modern condition, but he is not oblivious to literary tradition either: to fully understand *Gravity's Rainbow* one must be well-versed both in calculus and in the *Duino Elegies* of Rilke. The encyclopedic concerns of Pynchon make his books comparable to Joyce's in the amount and range of information they attempt to cram between two covers.

The Crying of Lot 49 is a particular gem because it is brief, economical, and possesses a deceptively simple surface. Its essence is ambiguity. As such it denies the permanence of the relative, and promotes the eternal quest for transcendence.

Pynchon indicates the main stumbling block to the fulfillment of the that quest in his use of the myth of Echo and Narcissus (thus we have Echo Courts, the motel at which Oedipa stays in San Narciso). To direct all one's love towards oneself, as most of the characters do, is to create a closed system, one that is highly susceptible to entropy. Only by keeping a channel of communication open to the outside so that creativity can flow back and forth can the amount of disorder in the system be held in check. Oedipa achieves such a flow between the Demon in herself and her conscious awareness, and she shares a flow of love with the drunken sailor—and, at the end, with all the dispossessed of America.

One sign of entropy is the failure to perceive distinctly a multifarious yet integrated reality. From the beginning Oedipa has this ability. When she drives into San Narciso, she looks down a slope:

> . . . onto a vast sprawl of houses which had grown up all together, like a well-tended crop, from the dull brown earth; and she thought of the time she'd opened a transistor radio to replace a battery and seen her first printed circuit. The ordered swirl of houses and streets, from this high angle, sprang at her now with the same unexpected, astonishing clarity as the circuit card had. Though she knew even less about radios than about Southern Californians, there were to both outward patterns a hieroglyphic sense of concealed meaning, of an intent to communicate. . . . she and the Chevy seemed parked at the centre of an odd, religious instant.[33]

This scene suggests a moment of transcendental consciousness along with a concrete perception: the world reflects back to the eye the same integrative and coherent pattern in which the brain waves are structured at that moment. Oedipa can see beneath the surface—not just of the narcissistic outside world with its entropic homogeneity, but of her own mind. Significantly, she is virtually the only woman in a book populated by variously self-centered and exaggeratedly caricatured males. Does Pynchon see in the Feminine the only hope for reprieve from the wasteland? The archetypal female in human nature is emotional and intuitive, qualities that the men in the book lack. Yet they also abrogate the archetypically male responsibility of questing. So Oedipa is forced to be a whole person, assuming both male and female responsibilities, to solve the greatest mystery—herself.

The implication of the last scene of the book, the auction, is apocalyptic. Oedipa, about to be initiated into the mysteries of Tristero, watches the auctioneer gesture like a priest or a "descending angel." Certainly that can spell no good for San Narciso and its inmates. But it can signal a release for the preterite—that is, the passed-over in every human being, the part of us that is ultimately free and apart from all surface insanities—invisible for its own protection. Apocalypse means revelation, destruction of ignorance, and what is revealed when the last veil is rent is the orderliness of pure consciousness, the integrated circuitry underlying all relative manifestation.

In an age when many have felt lost in a wasteland as bizarre as Pynchon's, as bleak as Bergman's and as inescapable as Strindberg's, it is encouraging to read the words of the *Bhagavad-Gita:* "Even a little of this dharma delivers from great fear." Dharma is the path of evolution, and the practice of experiencing pure consciousness is the most direct dharma for enlightenment. On this verse Maharishi comments:

> Just as the first ray of the sun dispels the darkness of the night, so the first step in this practice dispels the darkness of ignorance and fear. But although the first ray of the rising sun is able to dispel the darkness of the night, the sun still continues to rise, because its nature is not only to remove darkness, leaving the atmosphere dimly lighted, but also to shine forth in splendour and illumine the whole earth. The glory of the sun is its full mid-day light.[34]

Next we shall look at what it means to have that full midday light of cosmic consciousness.

Chapter 4

ENLIGHTENMENT

Juan Ramón Jiménez: *Poems*
Alexander Scriabin: *The Poem of Ecstasy*
D. H. Lawrence: *The Escaped Cock*

Transcendental consciousness is the source and goal of life: it is that oceanic pure awareness from which waves of thought arise and back into which they fall. It is as natural to take that inward plunge, to let the modifications of thought settle down, to merge the mind with the Absolute, as it is to have thoughts at all. The entire basis of meditation is the innate tendency of the mind to return, when given the opportunity, to its origin.

Why then, when this Absolute is realized, does it not stay? Why is it commonly experienced as impermanent? As Wordsworth lamented, "nothing can bring back the hour / Of splendour in the grass, of glory in the flower." The transcendental experience, though it comprises eternity, is as transient as a dewdrop.

Transcendental consciousness does not stay—nor does the meditator necessarily want it to. Most people have a world of things to do and relative desires to fulfill, a movie to see, money to earn, a friend to enjoy. To have practical fulfillment in life it is important to live both absolute and relative values. Each person was not born with peculiar talents and goals to abandon them in the quest of some monolithic absorption. But it turns out that absorption in transcendental consciousness, in the pure nature of the Self, is supremely practical for fulfilling those talents and attaining those idiosyncratic individual desires.

The person emerging from transcendental consciousness is impelled to do her work and enjoy life by the very force of nature itself. Plunging into activity, she is powered by the energy gained in transcendental non-activity, and utterly forgets and loses the value of pure consciousness. But as she meditates regularly over a period of time, something happens: the light of pure consciousness in meditation becomes less and less overshadowed by activity. The transcendental begins to overflow into everyday life until eventually it is there all the time, twenty-four hours a day. The fruit of this progressive alternation of transcendence and activity, Absolute and relative, is called cosmic consciousness—"cosmic" for its all-inclusiveness. The three relative states of consciousness—sleeping, dreaming, and waking—coexist with the fourth state, the non-changing, unconditioned eternality of consciousness itself, to form a fifth discrete style of functioning in the nervous system.

Cosmic consciousness, according to Maharishi Mahesh Yogi, is the state of fulfillment to which we are constantly evolving, whether we meditate or not. Nature impels us towards it with an irresistible current: all apparent denials of this higher nature are but temporary eddies in the flow. Cosmic consciousness is our rightful inheritance as human beings. But we can accelerate its arrival simply by meditating and living our lives; that is, by alternating the transcendent and the relative until they are indissoluble.

Cosmic consciousness is enlightenment; it is the stabilization of the fleeting moment of transcendental consciousness. In an enlightened person, the mind is fully, permanently awakened to its total potential of subjective expansion. The evolution to even higher states, discussed in the next two chapters, is based on an enrichment of the possibilities for objective rather than subjective development—a change in the world as we perceive it.

The state of cosmic consciousness is paradoxical in that one is in time yet out of it, comfortable with the boundaries and limitations of individual existence yet utterly unbounded in essential nature. One is a normal human being and also the essence of that which drives the cosmic machinery, from the atoms to the galaxies. Infinite energy and intelligence are at one's disposal even though one is confined to a physical body—not a confinement, really, but a unique and valuable opportunity to fulfill the cosmic purpose to which one is now attuned.

One of the most pervasive myths in Western civilization has been that of the struggle for freedom. The artistic dichotomy of classic and romantic, the political dichotomy of conservative and liberal, and all the various ideological and behavioral manifestations of this pair—to hold on or to let go—can be traced to this myth. Total freedom is what cosmic consciousness delivers. As Maharishi writes:

> When the individual consciousness achieves the status of
> cosmic existence then, in spite of all the obvious limita-

tions of individuality, a man is ever free, unbounded by
any aspect of time, space or causation, ever out of
bondage. This state of eternal freedom . . . is a result of
establishing the mind in the state of transcendental consciousness.[1]

Cosmic consciousness, then, is the fulfillment of the aspiration for
freedom—but not a relative freedom such as the throwing off of a political tyranny, the overcoming of poverty—rather, the freedom of consciousness from the overshadowing stress of human existence, which
truly is at the root of all slavery.

Yet the freedom cosmic consciousness brings is by no means contradictory to the classical, the conservative, or the Apollonian ideal of
order, for that freedom in unbounded awareness is the source of all the
order that exists in the relative world and that is transmitted by the
conventions of law, custom, ritual, ceremony, and tradition. To be in a
state of perfect freedom is to have no limitations on creative intelligence. We can act in perfect accord with the orderly processes of evolution which impel all towards freedom in self-realization.

The simple equation that perfect freedom equals perfect order may
seem ridiculous in light of the historic struggle between these values.
The pendulum has taken such violent swings from repression to
anarchy in social and cultural life that the two tendencies, each
admirable from a certain point of view, have polarized people, creating
warring factions, the partisans of order becoming tyrants and those of
freedom becoming rebels. Blake realized the self-defeating nature of
these warring forces and personified them as Urizen and Orc, fallen
aspects of man's higher nature, imprisoned by the single-mindedness of
their own virtues.

In cosmic consciousness, perfect rest and ultimate stability coexist
with creative energy and dynamic activity. The principle of harmonious growth, the root of all order, nourishes all fields of human
life. In it and nowhere else true freedom resides. Without its influence,
life is barren of all positive values and the selective championing of
any one of them can become a vice.

We need a poetic vision of the paradoxical state of cosmic consciousness, in which rest and activity coexist. Juan Ramón Jiménez,
one of the fathers of the twentieth century renaissance in Spanish poetry, expresses this dual nature in "I Am Not I":

I am not I.
        I am this one
walking beside me whom I do not see,
whom at times I manage to visit,
and whom at other times I forget;
who remains calm and silent while I talk,
and forgives, gently, when I hate,
who walks where I am not,
who will remain standing when I die. [2]

There are two "I"s: the time-bound small self and the unbounded big Self, who guides its younger sibling along the most evolutionary pathways with its influence of calm and silence. It orders life and yet is totally free from life's bondage.

Jiménez turns the ordinary conception of "I" into a "not-I" in this poem. The relative self is not the real Self. In cosmic consciousness we continue to identify with the ego that focuses consciousness through an individual nervous system, with the body and with the objects of our senses. We identify with the relative in that we continue to function in it, just as we did prior to gaining cosmic consciousness, but with one important difference: the participatory identification does not bind or restrict us to the relative. It does not overshadow the true nature of the Self, which is utterly free and unattached to the relative. The Self "witnesses" all phenomena from its vantage point of transcendental bliss.

This is a paradoxical state, as has been mentioned before, and Jiménez realized its poetic possibilities—poetry being the language of paradox. The image of the witnessing Self appears profusely in his poems. From "The Great Voice":

Solitude! Solitude! Everything clear and hushed now
Nothing troubling our peace; only a bell and a bird
        singing . . .

But love lives far off, serene and indifferent;
the fond heart is free yet, and knows no joy or sorrow.
Colors giving it pleasure: a breeze, a touch, a sweet
        scent.
It swims on a calm lake immune from sentiment. [3]

The soft, clear tones of the bell and the bird's song recur throughout the poem: life goes on, but appreciated on a refined level. The "calm lake," representing the detached Self, allows the heart to be freed from joy and sorrow, that is, from "sentiment." The unenlightened man is in bondage to his perceptions, either to joy in a positive stimulus or to sorrow in a negative one. The cosmically conscious man, on the other hand, is established in a field transcendental to those responses. And yet the heart here is not unfeeling: it experiences "pleasure," "it swims on a calm lake." The easy, enjoyable sensation of swimming suggests the nature of all activity in cosmic consciousness. This pleasure is something beyond joy, something that is innate in the nature of the Self: bliss. In every stroke of appreciation, the heart makes a wave of blissfulness on the oceanic nature of the Self. This pleasure is of a sort that has no relative cause and thus no end. How different from the shallowness of sentiments that come and go. This poem expresses the living impulse of this bliss in its eternality.

Jiménez implicitly recognizes that the witnessing faculty, that quiet aspect of Self detached from the activity of the ego, mind, and senses, is ever-present in the state of enlightenment. In "The Poet to his Soul," he says, "All night, you are awake / in your particular star, to life's persistence."[4] And in "Fortunate Creature" he celebrates a nameless being who goes "laughing through the water" and "whistling through the air"; it is everywhere, joyfully vibrating throughout creation, never eating or sleeping. This is no earthly animal. It is the Being of everything, which when we touch it transforms us:

> We shine, an instant, joyful with gold.
> It seems we, too, shall become
> Perennial like you,
> That we shall fly from mountain to mountain,
> That we shall leap from sky to sea,
> That we shall return, return, return
> For an eternity of eternities![5]

He calls the fortunate creature "The magical, single being, the sleepless being." Clearly the universal creature is pure consciousness, manifesting in all creatures, and every human being can have that inner wakefulness, even in deep sleep. This awareness is eternal; it is existence itself, outside of time, and can never be overshadowed by the vicissitudes of sleep and death.

Jiménez emphasizes the essential duality of the cosmically conscious state in "With Half of Me Yonder." He speaks of the transcendent, the "beyond-the-sky," "beyond-the-sea," as having come into his possession where he is now, in "the south":

> My silver here in the south, in this south,
> Consciousness in shining silver, palpitating
> In the clean morning,
> When the springtime draws flowers from my inmost
> self![6]

Half of him is "yonder," and half is "here in the south," where he possesses the completion which he yearned for as a child. In the "fulfilled joy" of manhood he has found "complete consciousness," and this is symbolized by "shining silver," conveying the luminosity and infinite worth of Being. Paradoxes are unavoidable; we must speak of the transcendental as no longer transcendental, as it is in a sense no longer "yonder": it is here. A person in cosmic consciousness can no longer transcend, because transcendental consciousness has become an ever-present reality. There is nowhere to go; there is only enjoyment of the wealth of Being in the relative world. The line "When the springtime draws flowers from my inmost self" actually indicates the evolutionary movement after cosmic consciousnss in which this inner wealth is spent or distributed to the sensory world, which then can be enjoyed objectively in its more refined values. I'll explore this idea further in the next chapter.

More than any other poet, Jiménez expresses the feeling of entering cosmic consciousness. A palpable quietness pervades his lyrics:

> I have a feeling that my boat
> has struck, down there in the depths,
> against a great thing.
> > And nothing
> happens! Nothing . . . Silence . . . Waves . . .
>
> —Nothing happens? Or has everything happened,
> and are we standing now, quietly, in the new life?
> > ("Oceans")[7]

This is exactly the right note. Cosmic consciousness is a coming into being, a realization of the timeless, silent background of experience that has been there all the time, which we have never noticed because it has been out of sight. The difference between ignorance and enlightenment is subtle, and it may be difficult to tell at first what has happened, or if anything has happened at all. Especially if one has been evolving at a quiet, steady pace over a period of time by alternating meditation and activity, the change to a new level of consciousness can be almost imperceptible. For it is silence that is growing, and silence makes no noise.

Jiménez frequently uses the sea as an image of the vast, internal ocean of pure consciousness. In the poem "Full Consciousness" he addresses the "god that has desires," which is "full consciousness" itself—the supreme power of evolution—from the "third sea" where the divine "voice of white fire" pervades the "universe of water." Formerly a voyager on a ship, the poet has his course transformed by consciousness:

> engraving for me with a blazing light my firm orbit:
> a black body
> with the glowing diamond in its center.[8]

The small self is as a dark mover, a shadow, irresistibly swayed by the centrality of the big Self; the contrast between light and dark emphasizes the clarity of the Absolute, its omnipotence and substantiality.

The expression "third sea" is obscure, purposefully so, to convey the sense of otherness. It places us in no ordinary waters. In another poem, "In My Third Sea," Jiménez seems to identify this place as the meeting ground for the soul and the Absolute, which is here identified with love, "the natural element which is the element / Of everything, the element forever." It is the recognition of the presence of pure consciousness that turns his world into a third sea which we might associate with cosmic consciousness. One sea may be the "natural" one, the relative world perceived through the senses; the second sea may be the transcendent Self; and the third sea may be the coexistence of Absolute and relative. The poem ends:

> Now I know and I am complete
> Because you, my longed-for god, are visible,
> Are audible, are perceptible

In the murmur and the color of the sea, now,
Because you are the mirror of myself
In the world, greater through you, who have touched
    me.[9]

"Touched" by the Absolute, the poet now experiences the whole range of sensory delights from the perspective of infinity. And as this passage indicates, cosmic consciousness is growing to higher states as the "god" who is the Self overflows from the internal sea and divinizes the phenomenal world.

In a haunting poem called "Being Awake" Jiménez describes the change in the quality of the emotions that comes with cosmic consciousness. The anarchy of disordered passions that is typical of the state of ignorance is replaced by innocence, love, and receptivity:

Night goes away, a black bull—
body heavy with mourning and fear and mystery—
it has been bellowing horribly, monstrously,
in genuine fear of all the dead;
and day arrives, a young child
who wants trust, and love, and jokes,
—a child who somewhere
far away, in the secret places
where what ends meets what is starting,
has been playing a moment
on some meadow or other
of light and darkness
with that bull who is running away . . .[10]

The black bull of ignorance and the young child of enlightenment: the contrast is clear, the desirable of "trust, and love, and jokes" over "mourning and fear and mystery." Childhood is a symbol for the regained innocence of cosmic consciousness, the bull is a symbol of the baser passions exorcised by this transformation, and the act of awakening from a dream is a metaphor for the experience of enlightenment. Will there be more nights with more bad dreams? There is no reason to think so. The night of ignorance has dissipated, the bull has been transcended. If the poem had implied that the bull was coming back, then indeed it would not be valid to call this a poem of cosmic consciousness, because there would be no ultimate transcendence from

69

the cycle of joy and sorrow which the heart was freed from in "The Great Voice." It is typical of Jiménez in his short lyrics to offer transcendence without qualification. We find ourselves quietly in a new world, and that's it. We are left suspended in the breath of the eternal from which the poet derives his inspiration.

In addition to childhood, Jiménez uses the image of nakedness to characterize the state of enlightenment. "At First She Came to Me Slowly" gives a more complex vision of the evolutionary process than "Being Awake." The poet describes a nameless woman whom he loved at first pure, as she was "dressed only in her innocence." He loved her then as one loves a child. But gradually she began putting on clothes and jewelry, blinding him with "bitterness and rage." Then:

> . . . She started going back toward nakedness.
> And I smiled.
>
> Soon she was back to the single shift
> of her old innocence.
> I believed in her a second time.
>
> Then she took off the cloth
> and was entirely naked . . .
> Naked poetry, always mine,
> that I have loved my whole life![11]

Here the awakening to enlightenment is more complex than the idea of a child waking from sleep, for the beloved one is a child at the beginning of the poem, in her primal innocence. It is only after she becomes corrupted, like a "queen" in her finery, that she can disrobe completely and be totally pure.

It is the myth of the Fall: like Adam and Eve, she loses her childlike paradisiac state and degenerates wretchedly into worldliness, only to be redeemed in the purity of the second birth through Christ; that is, through realization of the Self, or Christ within. Cosmic consciousness is a mature state; there is a greater level of purity in it than in unfallen childhood. It represents the victory of the innocent over the worldly, but with the added benefit of worldly wisdom and without the taint of worldly corruption.

There is a psychological inevitablity about the phase of worldliness we all go through when we grow up. The world is alluring; it is easy to get lost in selfish sensation-seeking. But of course the world is not inherently evil, it is simply *there*—a manifestation of the state of our minds. What is evil is that in learning to love the world we forget ourselves. If that is a necessary evil—a "phase"—it is quickly redeemed by stripping away the layers of illusion that mask the cosmic dimensions of Self, by seeing into the finite where the infinite lies.

Certain images reverberate through the poems of Jiménez: whiteness, the sea, the full moon, the garden, the rose, the naked body. In the silence and purity that he gives them, there is a whisper of intoxicating mildness:

> The moon goes by slowly,
> Naked, lovely, in ecstasy,
> Singing to an unknown earth
> Along her highways of dawn.[12]

The poet's images inspire a feeling for what cosmic consciousness is— a state of real life, not an intellectual mood that can be produced by an act of will. Its growth is natural: it is cultivated by allowing the mind to spontaneously enjoy the true nature of its being. It is the expansion of something innate that is continually with us, that makes us conscious— the continuity in our sense of identity.

This continuity is beautifully captured by Jiménez in "The Lumber Wagons." Wagons full of dead trees are going down the road to Pueblo Nuevo in the dusky afternoon. The oxen are daydreaming of their stalls; the drivers are looking at the sky; the wind, the trees, and the moon are full of the echo of these "crying" carts:

> The dead trees as they move
> through the calm of the fields
> leave behind a fresh honest smell
> like a heart thrown open.
> The Angelus falls
> from the steeple of the ancient town
> over the stripped fields
> which smell like a cemetery.
> What a sound of crying from these carts
> on the road to Pueblo Nuevo![13]

Amidst this mingled evocation of joy, sadness, death, birth, holiness, earthiness, dreams, work, of the quiet immensity of nature, of the harmony that interfuses all life, there is the continuity of the lumber wagons. The last two lines quoted above are repeated throughout the poem. What is the crying?—pangs of birth or death? The trees have been cut, yet they remain sustainers of life. The whole world is in the process of being reborn. There is "a fresh honest smell / like a heart thrown open," a purity of new life that is constantly coming into being in spite of pain and death. The situation of the poem is simple, mundane, an everyday occurrence, yet it evokes universality. The poet delights in glorifying the infinite continuity in the commonplace, the cosmic significance in every minute of ordinary life. Cosmic consciousness is not flashy or bizarre: it is closer to the simple awareness of "The Lumber Wagons."

If we characterize cosmic consciousness as blissful, then we need to account for the tone of melancholy in Jiménez's poetry which is as pervasive as his joy. There is an awareness of death, the *duende* that Robert Bly sees as characteristic of much Spanish poetry, particularly Lorca's. Paradoxically this heightened consciousness of the proximity of death accents the presence of life, of the luxurious vibrancy of the sensory world. In "Zenith," Jiménez asks death to join his life and make him entirely whole, to complete his half of light with the half of shadow:

> Thus I may be forever balanced
> Within the world's mind,
> At times the half of me aglow,
> At times the half of me oblivion—
>
> I shall not be I, O death,
> Until you, in your turn,
> Shall dress my soul in these pale bones.[14]

In this case oblivion is a consummation devoutly to be wished; it is that essence of Being, out of sight of ordinary waking experience, which seems dark, perhaps fearful. But the poet has faith that rebirth awaits him if he passes through death, that his consciousness of relative life will become "aglow" with joy if his yonder half can rest in the "oblivion" of the transcendent.

The romantic fascination with death has its roots in the evolutionary desire to make conscious the unconscious. Not all expressions of this desire may be healthy; the poet may not dig deeply enough or in the right place. The unconscious has its repressed horrors that are not particularly useful to resuscitate. That is why I have avoided identifying transcendental consciousness with the unconscious, though obviously it may be found there, buried in the state of waking ignorance. In Jiménez there is no question of digging for new, forbidden sensations, no fascination with decadence; there is only the quest for the diamond core of life which, when discovered, irradiates the common world with the dewy light of vision.

Death is part of the process by which life constantly recreates itself, and metaphorically the small self dies in the transition between ignorance and enlightenment. Jiménez sings of that best of deaths where the big Self rises from the ashes of the small self, and his melancholy is the sweet satisfaction of having tasted all joys and sorrows and of having transcended them. The vital processes of life, in their rich, paradoxical birth-and-death mixture, are given full play in his poetry because only they satisfy his thirst for completeness. As he writes in his essay "Heroic Reason":

> The spirit is immanency in motion and all the spirit conceives as life has to be movement, becoming, a continual being like the surf or the waves of the sea, forever new without leaving its waters or its beaches, and new because its waves change continually, because it is movement, and forward movement. The poet of the spirit, he who understands all men and understands himself (through a complete inner illumination which transcends and make the medium transcendent) is the only man who sees, orders, and controls every instant of life.[15]

In embracing the totality of change, then, we merge with the continuity underlying it. We find Being in Becoming, and know the identity of our consciousness with that undying essence:

> My beloved is none but the water,
> Always flowing and never deceiving,
> Always flowing and never changing,
> Always flowing and never ending.[16]

The equation of absolute freedom and absolute order posited at the beginning of this chapter makes sense only with reference to cosmic consciousness. To be fully conscious of one's own being is to be free of any impediments to the flow of inner and outer evolutionary change. When consciousness is functioning from the perfect orderliness of pure intelligence, one's thoughts and behavior are spontaneously life-supporting. This positive action naturally elicits a positive environmental response that facilitates the fulfillment of desires.

The music of the Russian composer Alexander Scriabin is saturated with the desire for this final, transcendent freedom. We can feel a Nietzschean striving for the Absolute in nearly everything he wrote. Scriabin's musical ideas were ahead of his time. He based some compositions on a six-note "mystic chord" symbolizing the primordial unity of the universe. He had a system of association of colors with specific tonalities and emotions (C = red = Human Will, G = orange-pink = Creative Play, etc.). And he was full of other concepts of musical symbolism. According to Faubion Bowers:

> Scriabin wanted the sound of the breeze through a pine tree as it would appear in a painting, or the look of a poem on music paper in sound. He considered music to be like prisms of crystals reflecting thousands of lights and colors. He strove to remove the human coefficient from music, so that all that was left would be purest, blinding, most radiant light . . . the light which man himself is when the "angel within unsheathes."[17]

His symphonies and piano sonatas forged a new musical language rooted in the romantic tradition but going far beyond it into atonality. Through sound he tried to extend the range of the senses to the ultimate, to synesthetic sensations and finally to the pure light of transcendence.

His final project, the "Mysterium," was to have been a multimedia "happening" performed in a temple in the Himalayas. It would fuse all art forms and engage all the senses; it would employ bells hanging from the clouds, brilliant waves of light and color, fragrances, dance and mime, tactile experiences, and thousands of spectator-participants. At the end of seven days it would culminate in the enlightenment of all mankind.

Despite Scriabin's boundless aspirations, his complex harmonic theory was extremely systematic and disciplined. Departing from the major-minor context of classical harmony, he invented something new and unique, "a total entity within itself," says Bowers. "He leveled the vertical and horizontal differences between harmony and melody to a single unity of compression."[18] His simplicity veils the complex, and authorities have for years been frustrated in trying to define his system because it is different from the way the music sounds. Thus in his artistry Scriabin developed orderly principles to support his lust for unlimited possibilities.

The current image of Scriabin as a maniacal precursor of psychedelica does not do justice to the visionary aspect of his art, which in its method was hardly anti-rational. With an understanding of his spiritual aspirations for "ecstasy" in terms of cosmic consciousness, we shall see that yesterday's madness can be today's science of creative intelligence.

Along with his fourth symphony, *The Poem of Ecstasy* (1908), Scriabin composed a poem which he regarded as an explanatory text.[19] Its hero is Spirit, which finds itself in a "magical world / Of heavenly forms and feelings"; intoxicated with sensations it prepares to sink into "oblivion." Just before this happens, however, it is revived with visions of "savage terrors" that awaken "Bright presentiments / Of shining rhythms" in Spirit's "divine will." Doing battle against the "yawning caverns / Of monster mouths," Spirit triumphs gloriously. "Fully delighted / With free / Godlike play," Spirit realizes its divine essence, fulfilling its highest desire. But then:

ALAS!
IT HAS ATTAINED ITS PURPOSE.
It longs for past struggle. Instantly it feels
Boredom, melancholy and emptiness.

To alleviate this monotonous condition, Spirit returns "to the kingdoms of grief and suffering" to confront the evil again, and to enjoy once more the rapture of triumph.

The cycle is endless. Spirit celebrates the necessity for endless change to support its ecstasy:

O my world, my life,
My blossoming, my ecstasy!

Your moments each by each
I create by negation
Of earlier experience.

By plunging into the cauldron of multiplicity, by giving up "to Love's thrill mid the flowers of its creations," Spirit "lives in freedom." The dark monster mouths which rise periodically to challenge Spirit's bliss are the unfulfilled desires that Spirit calls forth and then conquers by the principle of Play. Spirit calls:

"I summon you to life,
Hidden longings!
    You, sunken
    In the somber depths
    Of creative spirit,
    You timid embryos
    Of life,
    To you bring I
    Daring!"

Spirit serves as creator to give life to all the uncreated longings of the world. When Spirit liberates them by bringing them into consciousness, they gain freedom and Spirit gains ecstasy. The consummation is intensely sensual, and includes images of pain as well as pleasure which only further the passionate response. In this state of exaltation, every sensation becomes transcendently sweet as part of a single wave of bliss:

"And all of you is a single wave
Of liberty and joy.
Multiplicity has created you.
Legions of feelings
Have elevated you
O pure desires,
I create you,
This complex unity
    This feeling of bliss
Seizing you completely
I the affirmation.
I am Ecstasy."

The poem ends as the universe resounds with the joyful cry "I am!"

Being is the culmination of the ecstatic experience. The root meaning of ecstasy is "standing apart from"—a good way of describing the state of cosmic consciousness. When transcendental consciousness is imbued so thoroughly that it can never be lost, then "I am" is a perpetual reality which stands apart from but coexists with the ceaseless fluctuations of the sensory world. One aspect of life never changes, but the other never stands still. Forever identified with Being, Spirit can never lose the bliss that coexists with the changing world of the senses. Many meditators developing cosmic consciousness have spoken of a feeling of "witnessing" themselves passing through the relative states of consciousness, waking, dreaming, and sleeping. The freedom is such that every sensation, every emotion, even painful ones, are experienced from the level of ecstasy.

The urge for freedom, which is the impulse towards the ecstasy of cosmic consciousness, manifests in the multitude of longings and desires. Rebellion against limiting structures is in the highest sense a longing for perfect order; any relative structure can embody order only transiently and so must be transcended. In Scriabin's scheme, Spirit purifies and fulfills all desires from the platform of ecstasy. From his notebooks:

> In the existing order of things, protest and longing for the new order exist. Bust this is only a single rhythmic figure. In thought-form, ecstasy is the highest synthesis. In the guise of feeling, ecstasy is the highest bliss. In the guise of space, ecstasy is the highest development and destruction. Generally, ecstasy is the summit, the last moment, which comprehends the whole of humanity as a series of appearances.
>
> Time and space objectify this longing. Deep eternity and unending space are constellations around divine ecstasy illuminating it.[20]

It could be an experience in cosmic consciousness that the world seems only an appearance in comparison with the ultimate reality of the ever-present Absolute. This does not mean that the enlightened individual will dissociate himself from the world because it is "unreal." On the contrary, one is in a much better position to appreciate it. In Scriabin's poem, even "the serpent's sting / Is but a burning kiss."

Scriabin's philosophy has been interpreted as pure sensualism, that by drowning oneself in pleasures one can achieve transcendent ecstasy. That is a misconception. The Spirit in *The Poem of Ecstasy* can only know ecstasy when it seeks out "the new," when it uncovers the embryonic desires at the subtlest stratum of mind, closest to the source of awareness. Sensualists are bound to the objects of perception, but this liberated Spirit "kisses the joy as it flies," in Blake's words; Spirit neither binds nor does it become bound. And the desires the Spirit releases are cleansed by its all-suffusing radiance of any darkness that may cling to them.

Scriabin did not intend his poem as a substitute for the symphony. The emotional effect of the music is not at all dependent upon knowing the "program." At the beginning, shimmering strings, interweaving melodic strands of longing, rise into exultation, are met with the self-affirmation of the horns, and fall again into sweet submission. When an ominous strain develops, the trumpet becomes dominantly affirmative and quells the strings into soft, floating intoxication. The cycle of desire and fulfillment repeats, the trumpet riding giddily on cresting waves of luminescent sound and finally taming them. The piece builds dramatically to a climax in a major key. Suddenly it peaks, and there is silence. Again we hear the soft, melancholy violins, languorous and dreamy, and then the final "I am!" streams forth in a C major culmination. At that moment one feels the force of Scriabin's exclamation, "When you listen to Ecstasy look straight into the eye of the Sun!"[21]

Scriabin's mythos was that of the romantic apotheosis: the god-man, triumphing over all material constraints on his free spirit, fulfilling himself beyond good and evil. The limitations of ordinary men do not apply to him. This image of the hero as something more than human has offended many in this post-Nietszchean age. But we must look beyond the well-known perversions of the ideal to its real significance: the portrayal of a subtle aspect of human potentiality, the Superman in Everyman.

The Escaped Cock (1928) was D. H. Lawrence's version of the story of Christ's resurrection (this was Lawrence's title for what is better known in a slightly expurgated version as *The Man Who Died*). Here the superman is an ordinary human being, vulnerable and sensitive but strong; he is known only as "the man who has died," not named as Christ, though the identification is obvious. Lawrence's accomplishment is to give a credible representation of the god-man in all of us, and to clarify what it means to be fully alive.

The man who had died wakes in his cave from "utter nullity"; he aches all over, but manages to emerge back into the "animal outrush of light." Passing by the sleeping guards, he sees their "inert, heap-like bodies," the "slow squalor of their limbs," and feels disgust.[22] They are dead to the world. He has been physically dead, but now he re-emerges with a greater openness to life than he had known.

He stays awhile with a peasant couple, who shelter him so that he might not be arrested again, but they are boxed into "the little life" and are fearful of getting in trouble with the authorities. They have a cock that they have tied down for fear of its escape. They put the constraints of their littleness on its noble animal vitality.

The man now finds even his former disciples penned up in the little life. "Madeleine" encounters him in the garden where he had been betrayed, and this time she betrays him, although in a different way. She rejects him as he is now, an ordinary man, no longer the teacher or savior. He is indifferent to his former ministry, and she cannot understand:

> She glanced up at him, and saw the weariness settling again on his waxy face, and the vast disillusion in his dark eyes, and the underlying indifference. He felt her glance, and said to himself: No my own followers will want to do me to death again, for having risen up different from their expectation.[23]

Her dream image of the youthful messiah who encouraged her to give of herself too unrestrictedly is dead in this middle-aged, disillusioned, and self-contained stranger. He diagnoses his own previous messianic life as selfishness. He too gave more than he took, and this self-abnegating brand of egoism, he realizes, blocks the flow of life between people just as surely as if one only takes and never gives. The implication is that the Christian ideal of self-sacrifice, of turning the other cheek, is unbalanced. One has to look out for oneself, to know oneself. Indeed, Lawrence has proven himself very contemporary in rejecting the self-sacrificing, other-directed paradigm of love predominant in this century until recently. Current psychotherapy, at least, favors the ideal of the independent self-actualizer whose love is based on self-sufficiency.

In the first part of *The Escaped Cock,* the man is in a transitional state between death and life. He cannot touch others or allow them to touch him—"noli me tangere"—because he feels utterly alone inside his "uncaring self." He is as profoundly alone in the midst of the phenomenal world as he was in death, and nobody can understand that. His purpose now is to be fulfilled in that aloneness, here on earth. He has come back to life in order to really live. But others have already mythologized him out of this world again. He meets some men on the road, and they do not recognize him. He asks about the messiah, and they reply that he is about to ascend to his Father. Then he says:

> "Yea! And where then is his Father?"
> "Know ye not? You are then of the gentiles! The father is in heaven, above the cloud and the firmament."
> "Truly? How then will he ascend?"
> "As Elijah the prophet, he shall go up in a glory."
> "Even into the sky?"
> "Into the sky."
> "Then he is not risen in the flesh?"
> "He is risen in the flesh."
> "And will he take flesh up into the sky?"
> "The Father in heaven will take him up."[24]

They cannot conceive of heaven on earth, of living a fulfilled life in the flesh.

Lawrence commented in *Apocalypse* that "All religion, instead of being religion of *life,* here and now, became religion of postponed destiny, death, and reward *afterwards,* 'if you are good.'"[25] Lawrence substitutes the ideal of liberation for that of salvation. To want to "save" oneself is to hold back from the inexorable currents of change, of evolutionary flow and growth, to compromise one's present happiness for the sake of a narrow ideal of static perfection. What is better is liberation through growth of consciousness, through embrace of the many rites of passage we all must face. Any religion that does not make us better able to negotiate these passages is not a religion of life. Thus the man who had died realizes that to try to "save" the world does it no favor.

To want only "the good" is natural, but liberation implies transcendence of the good/evil dichotomy, and many fear being freed to that extent. It is safer to be saved in a second-class paradise. And for the man who had died, only fulfillment in this life satisfies his deepest urge for complete consciousness.

The disorientation he feels at first, the discomfort of the transition from death to life, is somewhat analogous to the period of entry into cosmic consciousness. As the man who had died feels too keenly his aloneness amidst the phenomenal world, so the newly enlightened person may sense the separation between the unchanging Self and the changing relative world as strange. Maharishi comments:

> . . . when Being first begins to be infused into the nature of the mind, the mind becomes as if intoxicated with a feeling of self-sufficiency. When the mind in this state acts through the senses, it behaves in a rather carefree manner, which may be thought of as akin to indifference. In a more advanced state of enlightenment this peculiar sense of indifference diminishes, and the behavior of the mind becomes more natural. Activity in the outer sphere of life becomes harmonized with the natural state of inner silence.[26]

The man who had died has nothing like desire in his newly-awakened state. He is disillusioned and indifferent towards what his life had been and sees no need to reassume the old role; but deeper in him than that disillusion is a profound resoluteness. And when he looks at nature, he sees the same impulse that is at his life's core:

> The man who had died looked nakedly onto life, and saw a vast resoluteness everywhere flinging itself up in stormy or subtle wave-crests, foam-tips emerging out of the blue invisible, a black- and orange cock, or the green flame tongues out of the extremes of the fig tree. They came forth, these things and creatures of spring, glowing with desire and assertion.[27]

This is the process Maharishi refers to: the growing harmonization of the state of inner silence with the outer life. The man who had died begins to feels the underlying, purposeful current of growth deep in his consciousness resonate with the tide of change sweeping through nature. He is getting accustomed to the state of cosmic consciousness, in which he is utterly "alone" in the separation of his Being from relative existence. But because of that he is better able to flow with the currents that connect the individual life with the life of the world. Paradoxically, the ultimate duality that characterizes cosmic consciousness is a higher state of integration than has ever been known before, just as from a lonely mountaintop one may truly see the wholeness of interrelationships in a landscape.

The man leaves the peasant couple, buying their cock, and deposits the bird in a yard where it can enjoy a large number of hens and yet not have to be tied up. Its proud, splendid aloneness is no longer violated by the constraints of the little life, symbolized by the cord that was around its leg. In the second part of the story, the man also enters into the fulfillment of his aloneness.

Here the myth of Osiris and Isis merges with the myth of Christ. The man who had died wanders to a temple in Lebanon where a young woman has become a priestess of the goddess Isis. She has identified herself with the goddess's legendary quest for the missing phallus of her husband Osiris. The priestess's father has been one of Mark Anthony's captains, and he was killed after Octavius took power. Now she is withdrawn from the world, waiting for the "re-born man," someone fully alive to relieve her sense of incompletion.

The man who had died fulfills her requirements, but he has not yet fully regained touch with the world and is indeed a bit afraid to "come into touch," for that seems harder to him than death. In the temple of Isis the priestess rubs his stigmata and the wound in his side with oil, saying "What was torn becomes a new flesh, what was a wound is full of fresh life, this scar is the eye of a violet."[28] As she massages his body, he reflects that in his previous life he had offered his disciples only the corpse of his love and not the love of his living body. He had advocated a bodiless, narrowly spiritual love that ignored the human need to commune with their whole physical and spiritual nature.

Imagery of light accompanies the man's final awakening:

> "On this rock I build my life!"
> The deep-folded, penetrable rock of the living woman! the woman, hiding her face. Himself bending over, powerful and new like dawn. He crouched to her, and he felt the blaze of his manhood and his power rise up in his loins, magnificent.
> "I am risen!"

Magnificent, blazing indomitable in the depths of his loins, his own sun dawned, and sent its fire running along his limbs, so that his face shone unconsciously.[29]

Throughout Lawrence's writings the sun is the symbol of transcendent identity; it is that primal energy source whose living presence in us can make us lords of life. It bestows a spiritual nobility: "The true aristocrat is the man who has passed all the relationships and has met the sun, and the sun is with him as a diadem."[30] This image is powerful and universal. In Plato's parable of the Cave, in the world of unenlightened waking life, only the shadows of things are seen, but the sun of pure Being outside the cave can illumine the mind to see things as they are.

When the man and woman in *The Escaped Cock* make love, they become identified with Osiris and Isis, the god and the goddess. They become lords of life, and there follows a season of bliss. She becomes pregnant, and the impending physical birth serves as a natural expression of the spiritual rebirth they have undergone. It symbolizes the tendency for growth and for transcendence of the limitations of the little life. Finally, however, the man must go away, as the Romans are about to recapture him. But it does not matter; he will someday return. For all time, the two will enjoy a union that no physical separation can sever. Established in complete fulfillment, they are not overshadowed by the varied experiences of union and parting life will bring.

The Escaped Cock establishes Christ as a version of the archetype of man in quest of cosmic consciousness. By dying, he becomes separate from the world of the living; he experiences the utter lack of connection between the relative and the Absolute. But following the progressive tendency of nature, he must integrate the two, and this means learning to maintain that separateness in the midst of activity. His resurrection in the flesh begins this process, and it culminates in his coming into touch with the woman. Symbolically, woman is the physical world. By desiring and loving her, he fulfills his physical side, which is, Lawrence urges, an integral part of human nature. Higher states of consciousness involve the integration of the senses on their highest level with the pure consciousness of the Self, and this is what the story is really about.

We might also see the point of *The Escaped Cock* as the universalization of the experience of death and resurrection in the sense of a process that is going on every moment. The old personality is continually being consumed in the flame that impels fuller self-realization.

This is none other than the holy fire of the Father, the pure consciousness of Self, the nobility of the sun in us, which, when we contact it, turns us all into Sons of Man, or manifestations of the cosmic Christ.

By representing Christ as a man who had a body as well as a soul, who was capable of knowing the tenderness of a woman, who could take as well as give, who had desires and emotions, Lawrence does not drag him down; he puts Christ inside of us. He shows that the spirit of religion is to bring the individual into full flower. God is within and the time to realize him is now.

Chapter 5

CELEBRATION

Hart Crane: *The Bridge*
Rainer Maria Rilke: *Sonnets to Orpheus*

In the previous chapters I have identified the Absolute with the impersonal aspect of God. The infinite, pure Being at the basis of all human consciousness is indistinguishable from God's essential being. This does not mean that man becomes God when he transcends. He does not become omniscient, omnipotent, and omnipresent. As man possesses a human body, his relative nature is inevitably that of the creature rather than the Creator.

Yet after attaining the enlightenment of cosmic consciousness, we evolve further to a state called God consciousness. This is not the same as having *God's* consciousness. But it means being able to see, taste, hear, touch, and smell the world on its most refined level. We appreciate the extent to which divine creative intelligence has lovingly molded all the forms of nature and connected all the endless minutiae of nature in a holistic, purposeful pattern, constantly evolving towards the ultimate fulfillment of every being.

Whereas in cosmic consciousness the mind grows to distinguish the relative from the Absolute, and thereby become established in Self-realization, in God consciousness the heart grows to find the celestial values of the non-Self. To gain cosmic consciousness is to lay the foundations for the house, but once the house is built and we can actually move in, the fun begins.

The foundation comes first. We must know ourselves before we can know anything else. When subjective knowledge is full, objective knowledge can blossom. Anthony Campbell writes:

> What happens in God consciousness, Maharishi says, is that these qualities of the Absolute, which in cosmic consciousness were confined to the subjective level, begin to

overflow into the world at large. Thus the world, as well as the Self, is seen to be filled with the divine.[1]

Or to use another metaphor, the light by which we see starts to glow from within what we see, illuming forms with the beauty that is truth.

Poetry seems the ideal language for the God consciousness vision. Hart Crane and Rainer Maria Rilke are two poets whose work is celebratory, suggesting an appreciation of life at its most glorious level, of heaven on earth.

Hart Crane was inspired by the Brooklyn Bridge, and he used it in his long poem *The Bridge* (1930) as a symbol of many sorts of connection. The two shores of past and future are linked by the eternal moment that the bridge, in its startling immanence, represents. The bridge is also the female body, the source and goal of man's life, which connected him to the stirrings of his inmost soul. It was the American continent, which sustained his westward quest for the lost continents of the mind. It was technology, the bridging of man's senses with the infinite beyond. And it was poetry, the technology of perception which could derive meaning from the husk of the twentieth century wasteland.

The desire for connection is present in all art that aspires to transcend its own form. Artists want to deliver more than a work, a production: they want to give an experience. In *The Bridge* Crane has made one of the most ambitious attempts since Dante to chart, on a mythic level, the architecture that connects humanity to the transcendent. The more he exposes us to the image of the bridge in all its manifestations, the more we feel that connection.

The Bridge itself is a bridge with many links. It is divided into a number of sections: "To Brooklyn Bridge," "Ave Maria," "Powhatan's Daughter," "Cutty Sark," "Cape Hatteras," "Three Songs," "Quaker Hill," "The Tunnel," and "Atlantis." These sections are wildly disparate in style and subject matter, but on less obvious levels they compose a unity. Certain recurring motifs and images suggest an imaginative voyage through time and space, recapitulating America's history and the movement westward, in quest of the mythic America.

Along with visions of this mythic America, we have glimpses of the wasteland that has no bridge to transcendence: the America of unredeemed vision. Crane's description of a subway ride shows technology at its worst: a tyrant that suppresses the life-instincts of the human heart:

> Dæmon, demurring and eventful yawn!
> Whose hideous laughter is a bellows mirth
> — Or the muffled slaughter of a day in birth . . .
>
> ("The Tunnel")[2]

The machine can be either a god or a demon. In the "Cape Hatteras" section, the airplane is alternately a symbol of divine aspirations ("Remember, Falcon-Ace, / Thou hast there in thy wrist a Sanskrit charge / To conjugate infinity's dim marge— / Anew!") and his self-destructiveness, for airplanes can be used to make was as well. Significantly, this section is a paean to Whitman, who celebrated the newly burgeoning technology as a manifestation of human creativity and expanding consciousness. That is ultimately the sense in which Crane sees it as well, and for him the Machine only becomes a demon when the Machine is invested with human vitality, thereby becoming a mechanical slave to it. The wasteland of the modern city is a state of spiritual inertia, symbolized by the commuter's continual breakneck plunge through a meaningless life.

If man's consciousness is dead, how can he revive himself? Crane's answer is to bridge the gap between the finitude of his limitations and the infinite source of his consciousness. If his technology is oppressing him, what can he do about it? He can expand his consciousness and use technology as an expression of his freedom rather than as an instrument of his oppression.

In the first section, "To Brooklyn Bridge," the bridge is painted in its visionary aspect as the symbolical merging of the conscious mind with its very source in pure consciousness:

> And Thee, across the harbor, silver-paced
> As though the sun took step of thee, yet left
> Some motion ever unspent in thy stride,—
> Implicitly thy freedom staying thee!

The bridge is a paradoxical fusion of rest and motion: it stays suspended, stable, at rest, because of its ability to move. The three great arcs of suspension cables that span it give it a flexibility that increases its strength, its ability to hold still.

Ultimate flexibility and freedom reside in pure consciousness. The primal energy at the source of thought makes possible all relative permanence, all coherent structure. The bridge's strength and flexibility are fused in this personification of the structure as a loving parent:

> Again the traffic lights that skim thy swift
> Unfractioned idiom, immaculate sigh of stars,
> Beading thy path — condense eternity:
> And we have seen night lifted in thine arms.

Here technology is humanized, even divinized, as a support to human spiritual aspirations. The bridge becomes a vision of the goal of the growth of consciousness: eternity. It also serves as a path to that goal, if we can use it as a medium to the mythic America that is the Promised Land of our collective striving:

> O Sleepless as the river under thee,
> Vaulting the sea, the prairies' dreaming sod,
> Unto us lowliest sometime sweep, descend
> And of the curveship lend a myth to God.

The bridge embodies a myth that makes God accessible to man. It spans the distance between the two, and under the majesty of its "curveship" is the vast continent, the mythic America, the world perceived in its finest relative value.

In the next section, "Ave Maria," we return to the original quest of Columbus for the land of vision. When he discovered America, he thought he had found Cathay, the golden land of the East. Columbus was not wrong: Cathay is the true spirit of America. While returning from his journey, he identifies the land he has discovered with a field of expanded consciousness, the Cathay of the mind, "the far / Hushed gleaming fields and pendant seething wheat / Of knowledge."

To pass from the Old to the New World, Columbus has had to cross the "third world" of water. It has its "gleaming mail," "invisible valves," "locks" and "tendons," a vast mechanical armor over a living body. He gives credit to Mary's mercy—the intervention of the divine feminine, a kind of bridge—for safe passage across this "abyss" of an ocean with its frightful hurricanes. With her influence, the ocean changes from a destructive menace:

> Some inmost sob, half-heard, dissuades the abyss,
> Merges the wind in measure to the waves,

Series on series, infinite,—till eyes
Starved wide on blackened tides, accrete—enclose
This turning rondure whole, this crescent ring
Sun-cusped and zoned with modulated fire
Like pearls that whisper through the Doge's hands.

No longer is the sea a threat; it comprises harmony, order, purposefulness, and wholeness. Merciful Mary's "half-heard" voice has changed that threatening aspect. The sea is seen in terms of its relation to the sky ("sun-cusped") and to the rest of the round earth ("this turning rondure whole"). This description is suggestive of God consciousness: in seeing a thing as more beautiful, one sees it more truly—as connected with everything else. Every object of awareness is a bridge to something else. It doesn't stop with itself.

With an understanding of the importance of connectedness in the highest vision, we can see why the idea of hierarchy was important in Dante's *Divine Comedy*. The Chain of Being, by which all creatures were linked on a continuum that culminated in the angels and God, was a "myth" or bridge that medieval man used to find his own connectedness to the Absolute. In Dante, each step leads to the next; nothing exists in isolation. Virgil is only a bridge to take Dante to Beatrice, and Beatrice is a bridge to take him to God. In Crane, the bridge's "curveship," its vaulting motion towards the higher states of consciousness, indicates an identification of roundness and connectedness. Every perception is a wholeness—like a circle—that spins us towards a higher wholeness. Indeed, Crane's image of "this turning rondure whole" recalls the many images of circularity in *Paradiso*, such as the pure white rose of the heavenly host Dante beholds in the highest heaven.

In *The Bridge*, the central symbol typically generates many equivalents. The bridge, identified with the Virgin Mary, extends further and becomes God himself in "Ave Maria." "O Thou who sleepest on Thyself," Columbus prays, and the combination of rest and activity in the images recalls the description of Brooklyn Bridge in the first section. God's own infinite power sustains his sleep, just as the bridge's freedom stays it, allows it to be at rest. The infinity and unboundedness of God, the silent Being of the "incognizable Word," is the ultimate aspiration of Columbus.

The trouble is that the vision will not last. "Still one shore beyond desire!" Having discovered Cathay, Columbus must turn around and leave it behind. And as Columbus's ideal of a golden land of lost innocence is itself lost as the country is settled, succeeding generations must continue his westward trip to recapture the visionary glimpse of Cathay.

The woman (Mary) whom Columbus follows is in a deeper sense his own soul, his Psyche, his virgin consciousness. The most subtle levels of the mind partake of the qualities associated with virginal youth: purity, energy, strength, innocence, receptivity. Dante's bridge was Beatrice, a real woman in the body, and just as concretely a force in his own consciousness.

Mary becomes Pocahontas in succeeding sections of the poem. For the first white men on the new continent, the historical Indian girl was a bridge between two civilizations, and in "Powhatan's Daughter" she becomes the American continent itself, the bridge by which humanity travels westward.

The poet identifies himself with some hobos walking down the railroad tracks (today's last pioneers traversing another bridge) and finds that they have contact with that feminine spirit of the land that is Pocahontas:

> —They know a body under the wide rain;
> Youngsters with eyes like fjords, old reprobates
> With racetrack jargon,—dotting immensity
> They lurk across her, knowing her yonder breast
> Snow-silvered, sumac-stained or smoky blue—
> Is past the valley-sleepers, south or west.

Good metaphors are effective not because they are convenient poetic devices but because they reveal a true identification not apparent on the surface. Here the land is a woman because in our soul, which is symbolically feminine, we *are* our country. The land we live in, that we have roots in, is intimately part of us. The archetypal connection of "earth" and "mother" is not accidental, and God consciousness intensifies our appreciation of this profound link between nature and ourselves.

The land is a woman, and she speaks in the language of poetry and music. In his quest for the divine female, the poet hears "the trout's moon whisper," "the singing tree," the "warm sibilance" of the llano grasses. He sees the "bridge immortal in the maize," hidden "On paths thou knowest best to claim her by." He praises the omnipresent goddess for her beauty and harmony and perceives the diversity of nature as a whole, comprising a greater body. As Columbus's ocean turned beneficent when seen in terms of a unity, so here the earth becomes a bride whom the poet can "marry": on the subtlest level, a divine bond bridges subject and object.

Pocahontas, the Earth Mother, is universal in space and time. But the poet has had to journey backward in time, imaginatively, in order to rediscover her virginal aspect, for modern man has despoiled her in his technological, urban civilization. This journey into the past is analogous to the penetration to subtler levels of perception in God consciousness: what has been buried emerges to be consciously appreciated.

In "Cape Hatteras," Whitman, the quintessential American poet, is the bridge that connects us to our original relation with the "red, eternal flesh of Pocahontas." Like the airplane which the poem celebrates, Whitman's poetry lets us soar above the earth, inevitably to return again, and thereby grace it with a rainbow arch. Like a young man parting from his mother to achieve great things in the world, humanity must leave the earth—that is, soar to extend its accomplishments in the objective sphere of life, but ultimately return to the mother lode of subjectivity.

Crane demonstrates how the outward urge leads inevitably to rediscovery of pure consciousness, the ultimate subjectivity:

> And now, as launched in abysmal cupolas of space,
> Toward endless terminals, Easters of speeding light—
> Vast engines outward veering with seraphic grace
> On clarion cylinders pass out of sight
> To course that span of consciousness thou'st named
> The Open Road—thy vision is reclaimed!

Whitman, in his "Song of the Open Road," described a vision of God consciousness in which the Self is unbounded and thus able to perceive with full appreciation: "my own master total and absolute," he said, "all seems beautiful to me." Crane invokes this visionary state by representing Whitman as the highest flier of them all. If our consciousness can soar as high as his, there is no danger of being oppressed by machines.

The artist's function, this section clarifies, is bridge-building, or myth-making. In "To Brooklyn Bridge" Crane prays that the bridge will

> Unto us lowliest sometime sweep, descend
> And of the curveship lend a myth to God.

The bridge will provide a link between man and God by becoming a myth, a manifestation of the divine that can be apprehended by man. If the artist can create myths, he will forge a similar link, as Whitman did:

> Our Meistersinger, thou set breath in steel;
> And it was you who on the boldest heel
> Stood up and flung the span on even wing
> Of that great Bridge, our Myth, whereof I sing!

Images of the bridge, flight, and poetry combine to equate all human creative activities, scientific and artistic. Crane's synthetic vision would not allow disharmony between what he saw as the noblest human endeavors. The final paradox is that in striving and shaping his aspirations into concrete reality, whether in the form of a machine or a poem, man reaches outward down the Open Road only to find his deepest Self. Objectivity, extended to fullness, takes one to the transcendent as surely as does the subjective path. Art and science, viewed on the level of God consciousness, are utterly compatible and serve equally as bridges to connect man with the source of his being.

In "Three Songs," Crane portrays the degeneration of woman in modern society. She has fallen from her mythic dignity to become, instead of Eve, a "simian Venus," a debased love goddess. Magdalene has relapsed to her original condition and is now a stripper at National Winter Garden, bedizened in pink beads, "silly snake rings," and fake turquoise. Mary is a virginal office worker in the Woolworth Building:

> O rain at seven,
> Pay-check at eleven—
> Keep smiling the boss away,
> Mary (what are you going to do?)
> Gone seven — gone eleven,
> And I'm still waiting you—
>
> O blue-eyed Mary with the claret scarf,
> Saturday Mary, mine!

Despite the apparent decline of the feminine ideal in these characters, there is hope for the rehumanization of womanhood because the poet can still perceive her underlying pristine mythic nature. The wasteland is redeemed by vision, the ability to sense the subtle essence. The beauty of God consciousness is that all things are seen in their best light, not merely the conventionally beautiful. In turning his vision to the sordid and commonplace, Crane does not despair about the collapse of the feminine ideal in the twentieth century but exults in the possibilities for renewal from within—where, in these women, their archaic splendor still resides.

The Bridge is not another *Waste Land*. Eliot showed the dead husk of the actual, the modern city in its immorality and chaos, spiritually barren. Crane shows the spiritual still alive in the actual. He shows less of a tendency to moralize about the surface deadness. His vision is not merely ironic; rather, it is directed to the positive qualities of life that may be discerned in the urban desert. Even in "The Tunnel," bleakest of the sections of *The Bridge,* after a chilling subway journey during which the poet feels the demon of the Machine has slaughtered all his newborn creative impulses, he concludes:

> And yet, like Lazarus, to feel the slope,
> The sod and billow breaking,—lifting ground,
> —A sound of waters bending astride the sky
> Unceasing with some Word that will not die . . . !

Because resurrection and rebirth are always latent within the wasteland's husk, even the impermanence of the moment of vision is not a defeat. When seen on the finest level, everything becomes a bridge to the Absolute. There is no need to stay fixed on one perception of beauty. The bridge is omnipresent and the poet must learn to seek it everywhere.

In the final section of the poem, "Atlantis," the ultimate goal is reached. The poet's fears of creative failure are quenched as God consciousness is affirmed as a permanent state. "Atlantis" is an unqualified, final statement of fulfillment on the level of the senses, established once and for all.

Having emerged from the night journey of "The Tunnel," the poet comes forth at midnight, on the bridge between one day and the next, between the present and the future—and finds the Brooklyn Bridge, which he left at the beginning of the work to seek other bridges in other times and places. Now it seems transfigured. Like the sunken continent of Atlantis, due for a new rising, the bridge is suddenly suffused with light. It is no static object; arching upward, defying gravity, it becomes a musical instrument, a harp playing music of prophecy:

> Through the bound cable strands, the arching path
> Upward, veering with light, the flight of strings,—
> Taut miles of shuttling moonlight syncopate
> The whispered rush, telepathy of wires.
> Up the index of night, granite and steel—
> Transparent meshes—fleckless the gleaming staves—
> Sibylline voices flicker, waveringly stream
> As though a god were issue of the strings. . . .

The cable strands of the bridge, like harp strings, sound forth in a song that is the form of the bridge itself: "One arc synoptic of all tides below." The bridge *is* that which it sings. And, by analogy, the poet is that which he sings. This final identification of the subject and object presages Unity consciousness, the seventh state, which we will take up in the next chapter.

The Bridge itself is an "arc synoptic of all tides below"; it spans the whole history of the continent; all social classes from hobos to pampered elite; all forms of femininity, Eve, Magdalene, and Mary, in their fallen and unfallen conditions; the many bridges of art, science, and love that are contained in the central symbol. All these crosscurrents are held wordlessly in the "telepathy of wires," and their juxtaposition turns to music, harmonized by the poet.

"Atlantis" is a poem of amazing concentration, especially coming at the end of a sequence where many diverse themes have been sounded. Here they are symphonically arranged in a network of words, any part of which becomes suggestive when viewed in light of the whole. For example:

> Onward and up the crystal-flooded aisle
> White tempest nets file upward, upward ring
> With silver terraces the humming spars,
> The loft of vision, palladium helm of stars.

These lines recall the "Ave Maria" section where Columbus has his stirring vision of "this turning rondure whole" while standing at the

94

helm of his ship. At the same time they also suggest Whitman's lofty airborne vision in "Cape Hatteras."

"Atlantis" completes the temporal cycle of the introductory poem "To Brooklyn Bridge," which begins at dawn and ends at night. "Atlantis" begins at night and ends at dawn. The intervening sections have, in a sense, all been composed of dream images, derived from individual and collective memory. The meaning of the experience is only clear at the end. With the recurring dawn, the disjointed quality of these images is softened. We see that wherever we have been, the Bridge has been there too, uplifting all earthly life with its overarching span.

In the last stanza of "Atlantis," Crane invokes the "Everpresence, beyond Time" of the bridge, which has now become, like the Son with the Father, the Word with the original Silence, the pure expression of the transcendent:

> So to thine Everpresence, beyond time,
> Like spears ensanguined of one tolling star
> That bleeds infinity—the orphic strings,
> Sidereal phalanxes, leap and converge . . .

The upright shafts of the structure are bloody with the life of the Absolute—"one tolling star / That bleeds infinity." The divine sacrifice, however, results in the joyful harmony of the bridge's "strings" in their humming exultation. The Absolute permeates relative life, raising it to the celestial connectedness that the bridge represents.

The concluding lines epitomize Crane's ideal conception of his own bridge, the poem itself:

> —One Song, one Bridge of Fire! Its it Cathay,
> Now pity steeps the grass and rainbows ring
> The serpent with the eagle in the leaves . . . ?
> Whispers antiphonal in azure swing.

The question mark accents the sense of wonder the poet feels at having arrived, finally, at the symbolical land of vision in which all his previous intuitions of bridges culminate in the "one arc synoptic." The serpent and the eagle, which in earlier sections were symbolically linked with the opposites of time and space, or male and female, but were not really reconciled to one another, are here harmoniously ringed by rainbow bridges of light. Those opposites, from which all diversity is born, live on in the "Whispers antiphonal." Rather than clashing, they make soft music.

These final notes are the song of duality within unity. All is not absorbed into the Absolute. As R. W. B. Lewis says, "Not the absolute pure . . . but the absolute inextricably wedded to the actual, seen and known by means of the actual even as it serves to transform the actual: this was Crane's regular purpose and his brand of totality."[3]

In God consciousness, the relative world is not dissolved; boundaries still remain, but the materiality of objects becomes less opaque. They glow with the light of Being. The actual is in the process of being transformed into the pure Absolute, but it is not quite complete.

For an earlier exponent of the God consciousness vision, we may turn with profit to Blake, who influenced Crane, especially with the couplet:

> We are led to believe a lie
> When we see *with* not *through* the eye.[4]

Blake saw the organ of vision as a window (or as a door, as in "If the doors of perception were cleansed, everything would appear to man as it is, infinite"). The clarity of vision depends on the cleanliness of the window. In other words, the world appears full of ugliness only if our vision is clouded by restrictions, the result of deep impressions in the nervous system. We do not see *with* the eye. It is not us. The Self is immaculate and apart from the eye. But the eye and the structures of the nervous system to which it is connected may be impure, causing us to see only cloudily through the perceptual window.

When we become enlightened, there is no longer a barrier to seeing the relative world in its celestial aspect. Blake's "A Vision of the Last Judgment" explains how one can feel apart from creation and yet, in another sense, feel closer to it than ever:

> [The outward Creation] is as the Dirt upon my feet, No part of Me. "What," it will be Question'd, "When the Sun rises, do you not see a round disk of fire somewhat like a Guinea?" O no, no, I see an Innumerable company of the Heavenly host crying "Holy, Holy, Holy is the Lord God Almighty." I question not my Corporeal or Vegetative

Eye any more than I would question a Window concerning a Sight. I look thro' it & and not with it."[5]

The Bridge culminates in a Blakean vision of a relative object transfigured by the light of the poetic consciousness. As Atlantis, the bridge has become identified with the lost continent of spiritual awareness, and rising out of unconsciousness into consciousness, it stands simultaneously for the enlightened subject and the celestial object.

Crane admitted to writing "absolute" poetry, evoking not "decoration or amusement" but rather "a state of consciousness, and 'innocence' (Blake) or absolute beauty."[6] Absolute beauty is what Keats was referring to in the phrase, "Beauty is truth, truth beauty"; it has nothing to do with the deceptive beauty of surface appearances. God consciousness penetrates to the most refined level of perception where there is no difference between moral and aesthetic truth. A celestial perception may be trusted because the celestial partakes of the changing relative and the non-changing Absolute at once. It bridges the two.

The God consciousness mode in art is basically celebratory. The artist ascends to a greater and greater appreciation of creation, and by the light of his refined awareness, all phenomena are arranged in orderly, vibrant patterns. Creation is at once fully alive and fully harmonious, thrilling with waves of energy and intelligence.

The artistic product, the work of art produced by the flow of the artist's consciousness towards the creator, is a bridge for the audience to participate in the creative current that brings both the world and the work into being. The work of art becomes not only a beautiful thing in itself but a vehicle for expanded awareness to propagate. It fuses beauty and truth, affirming the possibility for all people to rise to that sublime level of perception.

Rainer Maria Rilke composed the *Sonnets to Orpheus* in a couple of weeks during February, 1922. He had labored for ten years on his *Duino Elegies,* mostly in a state of frustration, when finally in a burst of creativity he was able to complete those long and somber musings on the human condition. At the same time the *Sonnets* arrived as a by-product, "dictated," as Rilke put it. The poet had served his poetic apprenticeship and readied the womb of his imagination for many years. The *Sonnets* then sprang into being through him like an immaculate conception—a classic example of the Romantic idea of creativity as a flash of divine inspiration—even more impressive because of the exacting demands of the sonnet form.

Whereas the *Elegies* lament the distance between man and the Absolute, and dwell on the difficulties and struggles of life, the *Sonnets* rise lightly above those heavy concerns to celebrate the immanence of the creative force throughout the world. But the Sonnets are richer for coming out of the experience of the *Elegies,* just as Dante's *Paradiso* is more profound for being the logical end of a journey that began in regions of darkness. The *Elegies* are explorations, hard, probing, tentative; the *Sonnets* are the joyous fruits of that quest, ripening effortlessly in the awakened vision of God consciousness.

To represent this level of life, Rilke uses Orpheus, the archetypal poet in whose footsteps Rilke treads, as a controlling mythic presence. Orpheus is the inner voice of the poet, an impulse very close to the silent level of pure consciousness at the source of thought, and he teaches the poet, like the animals in Sonnet I, 1, to be quiet and appreciate life:

> A tree rising. What a pure growing!
> Orpheus is singing! A tree inside the ear!
> Silence, silence. Yet new buildings,
> signals, and changes went on in the silence.
>
> Animals created by silence came forward from the clear
> and relaxed forest where their lairs were,
> and it turned out the reason they were so full of silence
> was not cunning, and not terror,
>
> it was listening. Growling, yelping, grunting now
> seemed all nonsense to them. And where before
> there was hardly a shed where this listening could go,
> a rough shelter put up out of animal need,
> with an entrance gate whose poles were wobbly,
> you created a temple for them deep inside their ears.[7]

The growing tree in the first stanza represents the growth of full appreciation on the basis of the subtle, silent song of Orpheus.

But why a tree in the ear? The image suggests that the basis for the expanded perception of the natural object is internal; that the growth of consciousness is as organic and natural as that of a tree; even that the technique of attaining that growth is through the conscious realization of the seed of Self, which by nourishment with attention grows greater and greater into the full tree of enlightenment.

Orpheus's temple is beyond the senses, but his music has to be bewitching enough to take us there *through* the senses. Once there, we are able to recognize the omnipresence of Orpheus as the creative spirit:

> Don't bother about a stone. Let the rose simply
> bloom each year in his memory.
> The rose is Orpheus. He takes different shapes
> in this and that. There's no need to worry
>
> about all these names. Once and for all,
> if there is poetry, Orpheus is there. He comes and goes.
>
> (I, 5)

Orpheus takes us into his temple so we can celebrate him in his creation. "The rose is Orpheus": praising the rose, we praise its creator. By looking through the form of the created thing we see the source of its beauty, the cosmic impulse running through it.

In I, 6, Rilke emphasizes that Orpheus's "deep nature" grows out of his knowledge of both the kingdoms of life and death. The mythic Orpheus, who temporarily retrieved his wife Eurydice from Hades by following her and charming the shades with his lute, knew that life and death are two sides of the same coin. Each supports the other. "He can bend down the branches of the willow best / who has experienced the roots of the willow," says Rilke, meaning that to know our world, one has to be aware of its roots in the other world.

Metaphorically, the kingdom of death becomes the Absolute in which the relative, phenomenal world has its roots. Like Orpheus, we cannot perceive enough of our world to praise it if we do not possess full consciousness of Self. From that basis, praise begins:

> To praise is the whole thing! A man who can praise
> comes toward us like ore out of the silences
> of rock. His heart, that dies, presses out
> for others a wine that is fresh forever.
>
> When the god's image takes hold of him,

his voice never collapses in the dust.
Everything turns to vineyards, everything turns to grapes,
made ready for harvest by his powerful south.

(I, 7)

Everything becomes enriched as we rise to God consciousness. As we
then press out the wine from the raw material of our senses, we are able
to express the praiseworthy essence from the most subtle level of relative appreciation.

Rilke's imagery suggests another parallel. Maharishi has spoken of
soma, a special product of the digestive system when consciousness has
reached a certain level of refinement. The cells of the body ingest this
soma, which facilitates the ability to hear, see, smell, taste, and touch
an object for its celestial as well as its gross surface values.[8] This is the
"wine that is fresh forever," the nectar of the gods on Olympus. Unlike
earthly alcohol, it clears rather than befuddles the mind.

In the myth, Orpheus was torn to pieces by the spurned mænads
and his head and harp were cast into the river where they went on
singing. Rilke alludes to this part of the story in I, 26:

> But you, divine one, you resounding to the end.
> When attacked by the swarm of rejected mænads,
> gorgeous god, you drowned out their shrieks with order,
> the architecture of your song rose from the destroyers.
>
> Not one of them could crush your head or lyre,
> despite their wrestling and raging;
> and touching you, all the sharp rocks they fired
> at your heart turned tender, gifted with hearing.
>
> Ravaged by vengeance, at last they broke and tore you.
> But the echo of your music lingered
> in rocks and lions, trees and birds. You still sing there.
>
> Oh you lost god! You everlasting clue!
> Because hate finally dismembered, scattered
> you, now we're merely nature's mouth and ears.

Archetypically, the dismembered or crucified god is sacrificed in order
to parcel out his state of consciousness to the world. In Chapter One I

noted that the Initiation phase of the monomyth, of which the divine dismemberment is a part, portrays the evolution to God consciousness. Having represented his establishment in cosmic consciousness by his Separation at the beginning of the Quest, the hero-god undergoes sacrifice in order that the objective world be raised to the same divine level as his subjective awareness.

Orpheus's broken body is thus parceled out into creation and infused into "rocks and lions, trees and birds." Ironically, it was the mænads' attempt to destroy the music that caused its widespread dispersal, so that the creatures of all times and places could enjoy the Orphic strings. A related irony is that Orpheus's dead body becomes the stuff of life, the primal creative impulse enlivening all the world. His body, broken by hate, becomes transubstantiated into assimilable love. In this myth the god's death is not an unhappy fall; it intensifies and multiplies the positive effect of his life. Evil turns into an unwitting accomplice in the overall goal of promoting evolution.

In several respects the Orpheus myth is ideal as a representation of God consciousness. Orpheus is on one hand the enlightened human being (or enlightened godlike faculty within man) capable of expressing the refined essence of the natural world, of praising it fully. Also, by virtue of his deep knowledge of the other side of relative life—its rootedness in the Absolute—he becomes identified with the creative impulse permeating nature. And as the sacrificed deity who redeems nature by letting the beauteous music of his awakened Self flow out and harmonize the dissonances of matter, he provides the pattern of the enlightened man who irradiates the world with the light of his own nature.

The things that Rilke chooses to praise in the Sonnets are by and large simple and ordinary: trees, flowers, fruits, animals, children. This accords with his advice to a young poet some twenty years earlier:

> If you will cling to Nature, to the simple in Nature, to the little things that hardly anyone sees, and that can so unexpectedly become big and beyond measuring; if you have this love of inconsiderable things and seek quite simply, as one who serves, to win the confidence of what seems poor: then everything will become easier, more coherent and somehow more conciliatory for you, not in your intellect, which lags marvelling behind, but in your inmost consciousness, waking and cognizance.[9]

If the ordinary fails to move us, it is only because we have become dull.

Simple things can be cosmic bridges, as when Rilke praises the orange and imagines young girls celebrating the taste of the fruit they have been eating:

> Dance the orange. Who can forget it,
> how, drowning in itself, it refuses
> its own sweetness. You've possessed it.
> Exquisite, it's been transmuted into you.
>
> Dance the orange. Discharge the warmer
> landscape out of you so the ripe will glisten
> in their native breezes! Glowing, strip
>
> perfume from perfume. Become sisters
> with the pure, resistant rind,
> the juice that fills the happy fruit!
>
> (I, 15)

The dance is an image of the harmony and orderliness of nature. Rilke uses it here to indicate that the girls have experienced the taste of the orange on such a subtle level that they have all but become it. The line "it's been transmuted into you" is in fact a statement of Unity consciousness (discussed in the next chapter). As the experiencer tastes more refined qualities of a food, he enjoys greater harmony with it. The "inconsiderable thing" becomes greater and greater, until finally subject and object are one. That the girls in this poem become "sisters" with the fruit shows that they have achieved what Rilke calls the "pure relation" with a thing as opposed to its possession.

This sense of relation allows Rilke to see the fragility of human life, a transient flowering or ripening that glows briefly and that much more brightly for its impermanence. In II, 7, the girls in their puberty are "wounded" like the flowers they pick. But as the flowers bloom even more when they are revived in water and arranged through the girls' love, so the girls will bloom yet more radiantly when they find the love that redeems their loss of childhood. Life's fragility is a charming illusion, as rebirth is always imminent in the wake of death.

The beautiful in life, like Orpheus who "comes and goes" between the living and dead, is in a state of perpetual transformation. Orpheus really praises his own spirit, the rapturous, singing, godlike flow of energy in all things, when he sings of the glory of creation. He makes the relative form transparent so that the divine light shines through its boundaries. The horse in I, 20, though it is shackled, hears the song of Orpheus inside itself, and "How the springs of stallion-blood leapt!" Its physical limitations do not prevent it from feeling the Orphic life-energy that suffuses it. Another beast, the unicorn, is celebrated in II, 4, as "the creature that doesn't exist," but which generations have loved anyway for that very reason. This love has given it life and has nourished it from the deepest level of consciousness, from which all possibilities can be realized. The creature grows a horn, a symbol of its purity and solitude. The artist too, by loving the intangible and operating from the purity of transcendental consciousness, the field of all possibilities, captures the evasive impossibility in his art, just as the lady in the poem catches the reflection of the unicorn's unearthly beauty in her mirror:

> It came here to a virgin, all white—
> and was in the mirror-silver and in her.

Praise uncovers the ideal aspect of a thing, its Platonic reality. The rose in II, 6, has changed its form throughout the ages. To the Greeks it was "a calyx with a simple ring"; now it is "the countless bloom, the inexhaustible thing." What we call it matters little:

> For centuries your perfume has been calling
> its sweetest names across to us;
> suddenly, it lies on the air like fame.
>
> Still, we don't know what to call it, we're guessing . . .
> And over to it memory carries
> what we have begged from hours filled with names.

The idea of a rose has endured and inspired devotion. That idea is the source of the beauty we may perceive in any particular rose. Because a flower fades so quickly, it is the perfect emblem of this ideal beauty. Its transiency reveals Orpheus, the celestial musician whose chords are most vibrant in that which is most momentary, for ideal beauty is not in time, it is eternal. It manifests in the Eternal Now and dissolves in time-bound awareness.

Most men, Rilke recognized, are not as open to life as the anemone flower, which in II, 5, he depicts as endlessly receptive to outside stimuli, "until the loud skies' polyphony / of light pours down into her womb." The poet notes:

> We are the violent, we can last longer.
> But when, in which of all possible
> lives, are we at last open and receivers?

Endurance in the relative world is not a value for Rilke. In the *Elegies*, for example, he finds some of his greatest consolation in children who have died young, their innocence unspoiled by life. The *Sonnets* themselves are dedicated to a young girl, Vera Knoop, whose dancing had moved him and who had died at the age of just twenty. In contrast to her presence in the *Sonnets* are the poems about machines, which Rilke consistently sees as menacing. It is not so much that machines are evil in themselves, but that men elevate them to spiritual entities to be obeyed. The real danger is in letting one's mind become a machine:

> It is life—it believes it's all-knowing,
> and with the same mind makes and orders and destructs.
>
> But for us existence is still enchanted. It's still
> Beginning in a hundred places. A playing
> of pure powers no one can touch and not kneel to and
>   marvel.

$$(II, 10)$$

Rilke is not so far from Crane, who saw technology as just another form of natural creative intelligence. Rilke prefers to celebrate the non-mechanical "natural." But he is not opposed to machines, only to people's tendency to turn themselves into machines and become hardened to life's creative impulses abounding in the commonest tree, flower, or fruit.

The person in God consciousness reveres the world rather than trying to "know" it. In II, 16, Rilke again invokes the image of the dismembered god who accepts and dwells in nature rather than confronting it solely as an object to be understood, possessed, and mastered:

> Torn open by us over and over again,

104

the god is the place that heals.
We're sharp because we will
know; but he's scattered and serene.

Here, in a reversal of our expectations, man is whole and the god fragmented. But paradoxically man's wholeness is "sharp" and thus self-
destructive, whereas the divine fragmentation is a submission to change
and thereby a receptivity to "healing" or authentic wholeness. Man
should be as if "dead" and drink from the well of Being at Orpheus's
silent behest.

Rilke's theme of transience as the true abode of beauty is summarized in II, 12:

> Will transformation. Oh be crazed for the fire
> in which something boasting with change is recalled
> from you: that designing spirit, the earthly's master,
> loves nothing as much as the turning point of the soaring
>   symbol.

"The turning point of the soaring symbol" is the *axis mundi*, the field
of all possibilities underlying relative manifestation. As Emerson noted
in *Nature*, the natural world is a symbol of a spiritual fact. Anything in
nature is symbolic if it recalls to us what underlies its beauteous display—the unmanifest, absolute essence.

> Whoever pours himself out like a spring, he's known by
>   Knowing;
> and she guides him enthralled through the serene
>   Creation
> that often ends with beginning and begins with ending.
>
> Every happy space they wander through, astounded,
> is a child or a grandchild of Departure. And the
>   transformed
> Daphne, feeling herself laurel, wills that you change into
>   wind.

"She," or Knowing *(Erkennung)*, is the feminine spirit whom we find
in the Sonnets as various incarnations of the young dancer—Vera
Knoop, Eurydice, the girls who dance the orange—and she reveals to

the poet here that transformation is desirable because life is self-regenerating. Everything is constantly beginning and ending, with each phase signaling its opposite. The bud's death is the bloom's birth, though no sooner has the flower bloomed than we contemplate its passing. If we, at Daphne's wish, change into wind, we will be part of the wave of transformation that flows through the world.

As Rilke enjoins us in II, 13, we should be so willing to change that we are actually "ahead of all Departure, as if it were / behind you like the winter that's just passed." The condition of cosmic consciousness, the radical separation of unchanging absolute Self and changing relative world, is a type of departure, an acceptance of the transient nature of the phenomenal world. This seems to be the state Rilke refers to in the next lines:

> For among winters there's one so endlessly winter
> That, wintering out, your heart will really last.

Rilke often conveys the idea of Being through images of winter, death, and non-being. This is not a contradiction: he is concerned to characterize the Absolute as devoid of all relative characteristics. Being "dead forever" in this poem means to rise in the "pure relation" of subject and object which is the state of God consciousness and the precondition for true praise.

The poet addresses the last poem of the sonnet cycle (II, 29) to himself—rather, to the Orpheus in him—the Self that dictates the poem through the medium of the poet's personality. Here Rilke speaks of the creative act as a distillation of the joyous from the often painful mixture of human experience:

> Silent friend of many distances,
> feel how your breath is still expanding space.
> Let yourself peal among the beams
> of dark belfries. Whatever preys
>
> on you will grow strong from this nourishment.
> Know transformation through and through.
> What experience has been most painful to you?
> If the drinking's bitter, turn to wine.

The poet identifies with the god's fragmentation. If one is sensitive to life, like anemone, one is likely to suffer the pangs of transformation, many little deaths. But by knowing the universe as flux and one's relative persona as part of it, one gains the separation that is characteristic of cosmic consciousness, and like Orpheus can nourish the physical creation by distributing oneself throughout. The sacrificial dismemberment of the god is only a metaphor for the expansion of every person to God consciousness. In that state, one sees the world as if glorified by the light of the enlightened self. If experience is bitter, "turn to wine": turn to the refined product, transformed through and through, of life's sour grapes. Raise experience to the celestial level where suffering is no longer found.

The wine is *soma,* the nectar that nourishes the senses at their subtlest level, their synesthetic conjunction:

> In this vast night, be the magic power
> at your senses' intersection,
> the meaning of their strange encounter.
>
> And if the earthly has forgotten
> you, say to the still earth: I flow.
> To the rushing water speak: I am.

The earthly and transient may ignore the poet. Worse, they may abuse him, as Orpheus was mistreated by the mænads. But as the river perpetuated his being forever by carrying his head and lyre, so in the last two lines of the poem the earth and the water uphold and validate the poet's state of consciousness. The earth is still, like the pure Being of the Absolute. The river rushes like the changing field of the relative in its inexorable flow of transformation. To the Absolute the poet says "I flow"; to the relative he says "I am." Thus human consciousness adds whatever is needed to nature. If it finds only stillness, it adds flow; if it finds flow, it adds stillness. The enlightened man embodies the two fullnesses, relative and Absolute together; he adds the integrative element to life however he finds it.

Rilke addressed his sonnets to Orpheus because they were hymns of thankfulness, appreciation and praise of "the little things" that make up a world, and that contain worlds in themselves. Like Crane, he was a bridge-builder, contemplating nature as a link to universal Being. The more transparent the natural object became, the more he distilled its joyous essence in his mind. Then the act of praise was itself a divine spirit, elevating him to the level of the god he revered, and enabling him to survey the world with an Orphic eye, in all its infinite variety of rhythms and currents of transformation. By evoking these elysian sensations in his poems, Rilke recapitulated the original act of creation.

Chapter 6

UNITY

Robert M. Pirsig: *Zen and the Art of Motorcycle Maintenance*
James Joyce: *Ulysses*
John Cowper Powys: *A Glastonbury Romance*

Here the journey ends. Here the journey begins. Unity consciousness: ultimate transcendence of the subject-object dichotomy. The infinite ocean of Being abounds in everything we perceive. We are one
with the world: people, animals, plants, the earth, the sky, the stars—all
are us. We take possession of a new universe.

The Upanishads deal solely with Unity consciousness, and their
constant refrain is that all is the Self. The youth Svetaketu is seeking
the ultimate knowledge, so his father asks him to pick a fruit of the
Nyagrodha tree. He has him break first the fruit and then the tiny seeds
within the fruit. What does Svetaketu see?

> "Nothing, sir."
> "The subtle essence you do not see, and in that is the
> whole of the Nyagrodha tree. Believe, my son, that that
> which is the subtle essence—in that have all things their
> existence. That is the truth. That is the Self. And that,
> Svetaketu, THAT ART THOU."[1]

When we search for the basis of creation, we arrive finally at the unmanifest, uncreated essence. One thinks of physicists splitting atoms
into finer and finer particles, searching for an ultimate particle, a physical quantity that is at the basis of it all. And what is uncovered is
greater indeterminacy, greater complexity. It can only end, if at all, in
the Absolute, that which we cannot define or break apart because it is
infinite.

At the point we become nothing—when we realize that our Self is
essentially unmanifest, and that the world which has seemed so real is
but an appearance of something else that can never be defined—then

we become everything. The Self, being infinite, is everywhere at once, as it always was and always will be, only now we *know* it. No understanding could be simpler or more obvious. The only trouble is that unless we are actually in Unity consciousness, the explanation is too simple to grasp. Thus the Upanishads have to repeat their message of non-duality over and over:

> The Self is honey for all beings, and all beings are honey for this Self. The intelligent, immortal being, the soul of this Self, and the intelligent, immortal being, the soul in the individual being—each is honey to the other. Brahman is the soul in each; he indeed is the Self in all. He is all.[2]

Metaphor, that magical fusion of opposites which reveals the unifying truth at their basis, is the only means by which Unity consciousness can be captured in words. "The honey of all beings": sticky because no one can escape one's own Self, sweet because the nature of the Self is bliss, and golden because the Self is the light of consciousness that illumines the golden essence of Self in all creation.

Words such as "monism" can never sum up Vedanta philosophy, for the whole is greater than the sum of the parts, and Unity consciousness is greater than any name attached to it. Unity encompasses pluralism as well as monism, for there is no loss of consciousness of distinction. In fact, everything is seen as unique in Unity, one of a kind, "distinguished" so thoroughly in its uniqueness that there *is* no self other than *its* Self. Everything does not reduce to a homogeneous oneness, a cosmic oatmeal. Rather everything becomes incomparably special.

Perhaps the Western tradition of rational analysis has felt threatened by the Indian metaphysicians' concept of *tat tvam asi,* or "That Art Thou," which seems to defy the significance of building systems based on making distinctions. This is not true; the philosophy dealing with the nature of Unity consciousness is itself a system that is compatible with other systems in the Indian tradition approaching reality from different angles. The different states of consciousness, after all, have world-views particularly appropriate to them.

A little learning can be dangerous; if an unenlightened man goes around babbling "All is One," he will be utterly deluding himself. That statement is not appropriate to his level of consciousness. His unity is the unity of ignorance, in which the Self is totally swallowed up in its identification with the object of perception. Cosmic consciousness destroys this false identification and separates Self and Other: the Absolute is one thing, the relative another, and they have nothing in common. God consciousness is the growth of the relative towards achieving the status of Absolute. In Unity that separation is finally resolved in a new identification of Self and Other. All relative manifestation is seen as the waves on the surface of an ocean of oneness. It is a shame that the value of the Upanishads should have been obscured by the misconception that Brahman is a field where logical distinctions are irrelevant. They are only subsumed under an ultimate Logos, the Word within all words, the Reason behind all reasons.

Robert M. Pirsig's *Zen and the Art of Motorcycle Maintenance* (1974) is an attempt to tell a story and fashion a philosophy integrating the Self and the non-Self. An semi-autobiographical work, it reads like a detective novel with long philosophical digressions. It is interesting in the present context less as a portrayal of a state of higher consciousness, which it is not, but more as an expression of the process that leads to ultimate Unity.

The narrator is riding with his eleven-year-old son Chris on a motorcycle trip from Minnesota to California. While they travel the narrator ruminates about the gap between romanticism and classicism in modern culture. These poles translate roughly to art and science, or the emotional, intuitive attitude of mind versus the rational, analytic attitude. He feels both have their shortcomings by themselves, but that if, say, his musician friend John would take the trouble to learn to repair his motorcycle, if the romantic would learn to understand the classical orientation and vice versa, society would begin to recover from its schizophrenia.

As father and son ride along, some shadows impinge on the author's awareness. It seems that another personality whom he calls Phaedrus once inhabited his body. There are few remains of memory left; the old identity was destroyed when Phaedrus went insane, was institutionalized and subjected to electric shock treatments. But now the memories start seeping back as the two travel through Phaedrus's old haunts in Montana.

It seems that Phaedrus was a genius of the classical temperament, an analytical wizard who consumed himself in a search for Truth. As a teacher of rhetoric he inspired his students with his fervor for a mystical word: Quality. He held that everyone knows Quality when one sees it, but that no one can define it. It is somehow outside the scope of rational analysis, although reason is utterly committed to the concept of Quality in its determination of values.

Phaedrus was frustrated because he was trying to communicate Quality inside of a framework inherently opposed to absolutes: the University, or as he called it, "the Church of Reason." The University was committed to a dualistic mode of inquiry, that of establishing an inviolable subject-object dichotomy and studying the matter under consideration "objectively" by removing consciousness as far as possible from the picture. The object was isolated, broken into parts, and classified. The romantic sensibility instinctively rejected this heartless procedure of analysis and perceived technology as a death-force. But Phaedrus was a classicist, committed to reason for the resolution of all questions. This was his downfall. A master with the analytical knife, "he took on so much and went so far in the end his real victim was himself."[3] This use of reason to combat reason inevitably put him in a double-bind.

According to Pirsig, true Quality is the result of an interaction of romantic and classical understanding. The romantic tends to appreciate a thing as it is to the senses; the classicist has to "understand" it through analysis. Technology as we know it derives from the classicists, but Pirsig notes, "The Buddha, the Godhead, resides quite as comfortably in the circuits of a digital computer or the gears of a cycle transmission as he does at the top of a mountain or in the petals of a flower."[4] The Buddha symbolizes the Quality that resides in all things when we see them with the expanded perception of a romantic-classical synthesis.

Quality is equivalent to what we have been discussing in this book as the Absolute, or Being, or pure consciousness. It is beyond all duality but is the source of all duality: all distinctions are Quality-distinctions. If we make a moral judgment, we are relying on an intuition of Quality to separate the good from the not-good. Even if we make a simple classification of the parts of a motorcycle into separate functions, we are defining the value of those parts in relationship to one another—a Quality-distinction. The very separation of subject and object is a Quality-distinction. By defining the boundaries of the perceiver who must function through a physical nervous system, we are defining the perceived limitations of the object which is grasped like a handful of sand from the endless shore that constitutes its total being.

"Quality is not a *thing*. It is an *event*," Pirsig concludes. It is an event that makes possible the awareness of subjects and objects that can be found only in the relationship of the two.[5] We might say the same of consciousness: it is an event outside the subject-object division. At the point of relationship between subject and object, which is not a part of either but is responsible for their equilibrium, is consciousness itself.

The narrator has to go beyond the intellectual formulation of the idea of Quality. He has to integrate it into his life. Phaedrus had been a genius on fire with his passion for Truth who could inspire others with his warmth and intensity. But he was not able to integrate his metaphysics with the physics of his daily activity. Teaching rhetoric in the university seemed a restrictedly rational activity in a rational setting, divorced from Quality. Towards the end he was reduced to a vegetable by the torment of this disparity. He found himself driving aimlessly through the streets of Chicago with his young son, relying on the other's imperfect, frightened judgment to guide them home.

Yet Chris remembers Phaedrus as his real father. The adaptive personality that has taken his place is a curiously spiritless individual, withdrawn most of the time. He seems to lack Quality. On this motorcycle journey, however, he is thinking constantly, putting together the fragments of Phaedrus's memory and philosophy and attempting to become whole again. The trip seems at many points a failure because there is so little satisfactory communication between Chris and his father. But as the father remembers more and more about Phaedrus and finds increasing evidence of Quality in his everyday life, the much-awaited healing occurs—at the end of the journey, on the shore of the Pacific Ocean.

Chris has been under suspicion of developing mental problems, and this seems supported by his depression and uncommunicativeness. But after the father's reintegration with the Phaedrus personality, he realizes that his son's only problem had been *him*. Chris had been "carrying" him psychologically, though physically Chris had been carried on his father's motorcycle. As soon as the personality of Phaedrus is resurrected, the boy's troubles dissolve and the current of love between the two flows again immediately.

The father's relationship with his son is representative of his relationship to the world, to the Other. Up until the end of the book there is an immense gulf between the father (the subject) and the son (the object). We hear about Quality in the narrator's thoughts but we see it too fleetingly in his human relationships. The son's antisocial symptoms are merely a reflection of his father's; when the father, who had adapted to the world and learned all about motorcycle maintenance, is reunited with Phaedrus, the original spark of Quality within him, then all other splits heal. The son's weight is lifted. He no longer needs to carry the burden of his father's struggle.

One of the most dramatic episodes in the book is Phaedrus's confrontation with the Chairman of the Committee on Analysis of Ideas and Study of Methods at the University of Chicago. Phaedrus's quest had led him to the Great Books program established by Robert Maynard Hutchins, which attracted him through its seeming concern for Quality. But the professors in this program, he found, were limited by their preoccupation with Aristotle.

Aristotle established the rationalist tradition by his separation of mind and matter. The subject/object dichotomy was inviolable. This prejudice is deadly when it comes to considering Quality, which transcends distinction. The great showdown between Phaedrus and the Chairman occurs in a class discussion of Plato's dialogue *Phaedrus,* which our modern Phaedrus has studied exhaustively in order to defeat the Chairman on his own ground. The Chairman sees Plato through Aristotelian glasses as saying that Reason, not Quality, is the ultimate principle, and he ignores Plato's concept of the transcendent "One," "the Good." But Phaedrus shows up the Chairman as a bluffer in his attempt to turn Plato into a mouthpiece.

In Phaedrus's eyes, Plato himself diluted the basis of Greek philosophy: the Sophist ideal of *aretê,* or excellence—Quality. The technique of Socratic dialectic, or rational discourse based on questions and answers, was set up as a higher good than Quality. The means of arriving at the truth became more important than Truth itself, and this drift was accentuated in Aristotle.

The University of Chicago episode shows that if we are committed to finding in the classics the quality at the basis of our intellectual tradition, we must learn to read them from a unified perspective that does not displace an absolute goal with a relative process. We cannot find the Quality in Aristotle by limiting ourselves to Aristotle's viewpoint as we conceive it any more than we can come to know the Self by staring in a mirror.

In Unity consciousness, the Self is all there is. Quality is inside us and outside us, but even though the body of the world is permeated with Quality, we can still make value distinctions. Unity is not a state

114

that ends the very interesting job of choosing between the useful and the irrelevant, the beautiful and the ugly, the righteous and the perverse. On the contrary, we become supremely equipped to make those choices. Here the journey truly begins. Once the foundation is laid, the edifice can be built. The concrete experience of the all-pervasiveness of abstract Quality enables us to know what events reflect it the most. Pirsig certainly delights in making such judgments: some particular victims are the dull people who travel along freeways in cars as opposed to those who brave the back roads on motorcycles. The eternal commuters are functionally sane but miserable because they don't know Quality. They have never exposed themselves, never emerged from their metallic shells and received intimations of Quality from the outside world.

The narrator is technically "insane" throughout most of the book. But here mental imbalance is a momentary stage in a progression towards ultimate sanity. The experience of a divided self, both in the fear that attends the split and the relief that attends the recovery, communicates an emotional message to anyone concerned with the evolution of consciousness—that the quest for wholeness is the most important thing in life. Despite the narrator's bizarre psychic upheavals, he maintains his trust in transcendent Quality, and that brings him safely into port.

In *Ulysses* (1922), James Joyce, like Robert Pirsig, portrays a developing holistic consciousness, but here we must search for the wholeness in a sum that is greater than any of its parts. This wholeness is not supplied too readily; it must be dug for, and it resides finally not in the book but in the reader's mind. Joyce presents a universe, the world of Dublin on June 16, 1904, and provides clues to the ordering principles of this microcosm. His world, with the infinite detail of life itself, extends into the world of our minds, which are forever forging new links between events, seeking new dimensions of order. The Absolute glimmers through the boundaries of this book as the invisible, inaudible, impalpable essence in relation to which the seemingly random and unimportant events of June 16, 1904, attain significance.

According to Joyce's friend Frank Budgen, the myth of Ulysses was the inspiration for the novel, and the realistic details emerged later. Joyce wanted to portray a "complete man," and, searching through literature for a prototype, rejected such characters as Faust and Hamlet, settling on Ulysses as one who was both father and son, husband and lover, warrior and conscientious objector.[6] Leopold Bloom, the Ulyssean hero of Joyce's book, is a rather ordinary, mild-mannered fellow who goes about his daily work of canvassing for newspaper advertisements while his sultry wife Molly commits adultery with the dashing Blazes Boylan. Bloom is so unlikely a successor to his noble Greek prototype that many critics have read the work as an ironic diminution of the modern man in general. For example, Bloom does not try to stop the adultery; in fact he deliberately avoids his home during the hours he knows Boylan will be there. Is Joyce implying that this is the best that our age can offer to compare with the ancient heroes and heroines?

I think rather that Joyce elevates the common man to the mythic level by the comparison. Bloom's peregrinations about Dublin to various pubs and businesses are perhaps on the surface a diminution of Ulysses' adventures on the islands where he stopped on his way to Ithaca. But deep within the literal events of *Ulysses* is buried the mythic pattern, just as it is in every day of our lives. Each of us is the "complete man," the *anthropos,* archetype of the higher Self. We each contain the potential for completeness in that we exist as human beings, thereby participating in cosmic Being. In Indian philosophy this original Being is named Purusha (literally, "person"), and we have his equivalents in the West, Adam, Albion (in Blake), and H. C. Earwicker in Joyce's *Finnegans Wake* (H. C. E. = Here Comes Everybody). The myth of the original ancestor of the human race signifies that our consciousness, down at its deepest origin, is complete. It is the seed that generates our sense of identity and our desires to make conscious the intuited inner completeness.

The traditional role of the hero is that of pure consciousness moving through space and time and redeeming the imperfections of the relative world. His mere presence in the world indicates the structure of Unity consciousness, where the Absolute is found in the relative. To see this dimension in *Ulysses* we must look through the realistic level of detail and discern the mythic lineaments. Richard Ellmann does this by discussing Bloom's Ulyssean mastery of words:

> Bloom has to speak in ordinary language, untrained by anything but natural ingenuity, relaxed rather than tense, not so fastidious as to be above the most wellworn expressions, yet skeptical of them, even taking a keen pleasure in maneuvering among common idioms, allu-

sions, and proverbs. It is this power of speech, mostly inward speech, that inclines Bloom towards Odysseus—
resilience, the power to recoup in the mind what he loses
in the flesh.[7]

Joyce used stream-of-consciousness technique to penetrate to a subtler
and richer level of language than outward speech. Furthermore, in that
Bloom represents Logos, or the Word beyond all words, his inward
speech takes us closer to the essence of all things.

Logos, which comes from the Greek verb *lego,* "I say," was in
Heraclitus's philosophy the rational governing principle of the universe
immanent in creation. The universe is, as it were, *spoken* by the supreme intelligence of Logos, and Logos is also the expression of that
intelligence, the vibrating individual consciousness of rocks, trees,
animals, and people. In the Gospel of St. John, Logos is the Word that
is with God and is God—that is, Christ as manifested expression of the
ultimate unmanifest source of creation. As Rudolph Steiner interprets
the concept: "The lily-of-the-valley produces the seed and the seed
again the lily-of-the-valley; in like manner the divine creative Word
created the mute human seed—and when this primeval creative Word
had glided into the human seed, in order to spring up again within it, it
sounded forth in words."[8] Bloom is associated with Christ at many
points as when he floats in the morning bath thinking "This is my
body." As Ellman explains, "Joyce prefers the human form divine to
the divine form human."[9] The greatest miracle is life in its earthly
vestments, experienced fully through the senses. Bloom at every turn
reveals the Logos in matter, the Word springing up in the human seed.

Joyce rejects otherworldly religion. Catholicism and theosophy
alike are mocked in *Ulysses* as life-denying. Joyce in his personal religion sacralizes the world, attending to what Blake called the "Minute
Particulars." *Ulysses,* in its exhaustive realism, transcends the literal
fact for the sacred fact saturated with infinity.

Bloom then is the Logos, the divine creative principle. He travels
through the world and everywhere he discovers Logos. Matter becomes
alive for him, and as the embodied Word he gives expression to the
mute universe. In the "Hades" episode, at a funeral, he considers the
question of physical resurrection and decides the conventional view is
ridiculous. An acquaintance utters the pious platitude, "I am the resurrection and the life. That touches a man's inmost heart." Bloom thinks:

Your heart perhaps but what price the fellow in the six feet by two with his toes to the daisies? No touching that. Seat of the affections. Broken heart. A pump after all, pumping thousands of gallons of blood every day. One fine day it gets bunged up and there you are. Lots of them lying around here: lungs, hearts, livers. Old rusty pumps: damn the thing else. The resurrection and the life. Once you are dead you are dead. That last day idea. Knocking them all up out of their graves. Come forth, Lazarus! And he came fifth and lost the job. Get up! Last day! Then every fellow mousing around for his liver and his lights and the rest of his traps.[10]

Bloom does not idealize or spiritualize matter. He sees it for what it is—a container for the life-essence, complete now in the natural fact and not in some future spiritualized state. Bloom continually resurrects the dead in his thoughts. He gives life to whatever he perceives, penetrating to the Logos of the matter.

Bloom is the "complete man": in him is the Logos in its immanence, the Word made flesh, and also in its transcendence as pure consciousness. He is at once a transcendental witness to the events of the day and a participant in them, who can shape them to good ends in an effortless manner. For example, whereas Ulysses had to slay the suitors of Penelope with his bow, Bloom achieves a similar purpose by doing nothing. He leaves Molly to dally all day and finally returns to her bed in the middle of the night. Then we find, in her sleepy ruminations, that Boylan is sinking in her favor and her husband is rising. Her thoughts culminate in the memory of her first lovemaking with Bloom, and the novel ends with her acceptance of him, "and yes I said yes I will Yes."[11] The outcome may be seen as tentative because this is the story of just one day. Still, this modern Ulysses has succeeded in defeating his wife's suitor.

Bloom's seeming passivity is his greatest strength and the mark of his completeness. He is something of an androgyne, embodying characteristics of both the archetypal male and female, and is thus a living Tao. He represents both Yang, the active male force, associated with the sky, light, and the urge to explore and discover, and also Yin, the female, the passive earth, the dark, the centrality of the womb. One passage refers to "the surety of the sense of touch in his firm full masculine feminine passive active hand."[12] Bloom has a gentle nature and

118

takes delight in the physical, but he also has a masculine scientific bent and an analytical temperament. This balance is quite in keeping with his role as Logos, for the Logos is associated in certain traditions with androgyny. According to Mircea Eliade, Christ was thought androgynous by some Christian sects, as was Adam. Furthermore, Adam-Christ was the *anthropos* existing potentially in every human being:

> Simon Magus called the primordial spirit *arsenothelys,* "male-female." The Naasenes also imagined the celestial Man, Adamas, as an *arsenothelys.* Terrestrial Adam was no more an image of the celestial archetype; he too, therefore, was an androgyne. By the fact that the human race descends from Adam, the *arsenothelys* exists virtually in every man, and spiritual perfection consists precisely in rediscovering within oneself this androgynous nature. The supreme Spirit, the Logos, was itself androgynous also. . . . According to the Naasenes, the cosmic drama contains three elements: (1) the pre-existent Logos as a divine and universal totality; (2) the Fall, which caused the break-up of Creation and the birth of suffering; (3) the coming of the Saviour who by his unity reintegrated the countless fragments which make up our present-day Universe. According to the Naasenes, androgyny is one moment in a vast process of cosmic unification.[13]

Bloom in his androgynous completeness represents both the Logos incarnate and the transcendental pre-existent Logos. As Son, as immanent messiah, he implants the seminal Word in the speechless fallen world, from which he also maintains a paternal, transcendent detachment. And both of these male roles are fulfilled through a sympathy with the feminine. In the phantasmagoric "Circe" episode, Bloom changes into a woman and is proclaimed as "a finished example of the new womanly man."[14] In this instance Bloom's womanliness is shown as a weakness, though from the point of view of the symbolism of androgyny, it actually indicates his secret strength. As Molly says of him at the end, "that was why I liked him because I saw he understood or felt what a woman is and I knew I could always get round him . . ."[15] Molly responds to the androgynous completeness in his nature.

As the masculine-feminine Tao, as the transcendent-immanent Logos, as the Ulyssean "complete man," Bloom himself is a microcosm. But Joyce's work contains many levels, and in *Ulysses* the archetypal nuclear family, Father, Mother, and Son, all contained *in* Bloom, are also represented by the relationship of Bloom, Molly, and the young artist Stephen Dedalus. Stephen is not their natural son but they become in a sense his spiritual parents in the course of the novel. He has no connection with his biological parents and even refuses to fulfill his mother's dying request to kneel by her bedside and pray. He is alienated from family and friends. His job as a schoolteacher confines him to the trodden paths of pedagogy, and though he extemporizes brilliantly on Shakespeare in a literary gathering, he is not taken seriously as a writer by the established literati. As Telemachus, he searches for his father Ulysses without knowing it. Atonement with the Father is one of the great mythic themes. According to Joseph Campbell, in the traditional idea of initiation, "the father is initiating priest through whom the young being passes on into the larger world."[16] To be initiated is to be spiritually reborn, and Stephen must achieve this rebirth if he is to take his place confidently as an artist, assuming the nature of the Logos and delivering the Word to his fellow man.

Bloom as well as Stephen experiences a rebirth through their encounter in accordance with the classic pattern of the initiation, in which, as Campbell puts it, "We are taken from the mother, chewed into fragments and assimilated to the world-annihilating body of the ogre for whom all the precious forms and beings are only the courses of a feast; but then, miraculously reborn, we are more than we were."[17] Both Bloom and Stephen have experienced a separation from the female. Stephen has been alienated from his mother and conceives of Woman as "allwombing tomb,"[18] a Death Mother. For him the sea is an image of this destructive feminine power, and he avoids swimming in it. Bloom is also alienated from Woman in his own way. He has left Molly at home for the day though knowing of her intended infidelity, and he engages in some furtive and ineffectual infidelities of his own (writing a suggestive letter to a "pen pal"; masturbating while watching an adolescent girl on the beach). Both Stephen and Bloom are "annihilated," or subjected to various humiliations throughout the day, as when Bloom in the "Lestrygonians" episode feels "as if I had been eaten and spewed" in his disgust with the crudity and dullness of people at lunchtime.[19] The peak of this annihilation occurs in the "Circe" episode, where Stephen and Bloom find themselves in Dublin's Nighttown, confronting personified fragments of their psyches. The intense catharsis of coming to terms with their split personalities prepares them for "rebirth."

Their souls have parched and cracked from lack of the female water, and they must pass though the Woman in order to be whole again. So Bloom returns finally to his wife, taking Stephen with him. He has shown Stephen a photograph of Molly, and her presence back in the "Ithaca" of the Bloom residence at 7 Eccles Street attracts them both. Although she has gone to bed, the very fact that they are in her domain puts them under her harmonizing, reconciling female influence. Archetypically, the home itself is a female entity; it is a point of rest amidst the activity of the world, a womb.

After sharing a symbolic communion of cocoa, Bloom and Stephen talk and develop their relationship. Bloom is a kind of scientist in his rootedness to sensory reality, and he tells the artist Stephen of some of his projected inventions and ideas for the betterment of mankind. Stephen recites poetry and discusses linguistics and philosophy. Each is exposed to the other's bias and becomes more complete. They find a healing from the night's schizophrenia in a union as father and son. Together, at this moment, they are comprised in a wholeness. Stephen hears in Bloom's voice the "profound ancient male unfamiliar melody" of the past, and Bloom sees in the "quick young male" the "predestination of a future."[20] Youth and maturity in sympathetic communication elevate the value of the present moment by filling it with the values of time past and time future, experience and vision. This heightened sense of the moment culminates at their separation, when they go out into the garden and behold "The heaventree of stars hung with humid nightblue fruit." Accompanying this vision are "Meditations of evolution increasingly vaster"; Bloom considers the immeasurable interstellar distances and the "infinitely remote futures in comparison with which the years, threescore and ten, of allotted human life formed a parenthesis of infinitesimal brevity."[21]

The Father has brought the Son back into touch with concrete reality, and the two have nourished each other on their opposite natures. Now Stephen is replete with the paternal Logos, and we can expect him to start to fulfill his artistic aspirations in giving mature expression of his Word. The vision of the heaventree of stars has sealed their union with sacral import whether or not they ever meet again. It is the moment that is important. As Stephen said earlier in the novel, God is "a shout in the street," an immanent presence.[22]

After Stephen's departure, Bloom achieves a reconciliation of sorts with the other person of the trinity, Molly. It is the female spirit that has brought the two men together, and it is the son who restores the harmony between the parents. In the long internal monologue that closes *Ulysses,* Molly, lying in bed after Bloom's return, reflects on the faults and virtues of Bloom and Boylan, with Bloom coming off rather badly at first. But then her thoughts turn to Stephen. Although she does not know him, she begins to fantasize a romance. As a sensitive, intelligent, poetic youth, he stirs her passion. Compared to Stephen, the satyr Boylan seems crude. But her thoughts soon return to Bloom, and as if strengthened by his association with Stephen, he finds more favor in her judgment. Finally it is clear that Bloom has triumphed over his rival. Though he didn't use a long bow to accomplish it, what Bloom did do was forgive and forget: before falling asleep, "He kissed the plump mellow yellow smellow melons of her rump."[23] In the words of Harry Blamires, "the kisses represent his decisive and final Yes."[24]

Molly's monologue is above all earthy, appropriately so, as she is compared to the Earth Mother Gea-Tellus as she lies on the bed. The feminine archetype is Nature herself, and Molly's preoccupation with sex is the pure expression of the life force following its natural tendency through the physical world. By sacralizing the earthly, she is a goddess of nature, especially when she recalls the day that she and Bloom first made love:

> O that awful deepdown torrent O and the sea the sea crimson sometimes like fire and the glorious sunsets and the figtrees in the Alameda gardens yes and all the queer little streets and pink and blue and yellow houses and the rosegardens and the jessamine and geraniums and cactuses and Gibraltar as a girl where I was A Flower of the mountain yes . . .[25]

Molly has a simple belief in God based on the overwhelming plenitude of nature. For her God is always immanent and redeems the sorrow of life by continual, joyful replenishment. There is little room for distinctions between the sacred and the profane here. All opposites are subsumed under the cosmic unitive eye of Molly.

We do not know whether Bloom and his wife will reconcile their differences come the morning of June 17, 1904 (they have not made love in ten years). The future is tentative. But this day of *Ulysses* has been a turning point of some kind, filled with mythic implications for spiritual rebirth. Joyce has distilled a moment of individual life, unimaginably brief against the life of the stars, and shown it to be infinitely precious, to contain a universe within its tiny compass. The Absolute is with us now, in that shout from the street, and the fulfillment of consciousness is the realization of the constant field of infinite life that permeates the rich and endlessly detailed mosaic of our everyday world.

A Glastonbury Romance (1933), by John Cowper Powys, is an underappreciated masterpiece that has, in fact, been out of print for a number of years. Yet J. D. Beresford, Colin Wilson, and other important critics have ranked it among the great novels of the world. Its opening paragraph is daunting:

> At the striking of noon on a certain fifth of March, there occurred within a causal radius of Brandon railway station and yet beyond the deepest pools of emptiness between the uttermost stellar systems one of those infinitesimal ripples in the creative silence of the First Cause which always occur when an exceptional stir of heightened consciousness agitates any living organism in this astronomical universe. Something passed at that moment, a wave, a motion, a vibration, too tenuous to be called magnetic, too subliminal to be called spiritual, between the soul of a particular human being who was emerging from a third-class carriage of the twelve-nineteen train from London and the divine-diabolic soul of the First Cause of all life.[26]

What follows, for a half-million words, is a fusion of the "realistic" with the cosmic. The story renders the infinite minute particulars of everyday human life in terms of their relationship to the life of everything else in the universe, from stones, vegetation, insects, and animal life to heavenly bodies and superhuman entities. There are forty-eight characters whose paths intersect in countless combinations, whose relationships are more complex and more subtle then they themselves can imagine. The world of Glastonbury is a microcosm of humanity. Most of the various philosophies and approaches to life may be found—stoic, epicurean, orthodox Christian, existentialist, atheist, materialist, mystic, aesthetic, and so on; aristocrats, communists, capitalists, and anarchists mix it up; people of all ages and personalities undergo birth and death, passion and spirituality, insanity and transcendence.

The novel is encyclopedic but in a different way than *Ulysses*. Whereas Joyce seems to include everything about Dublin (and through allusion, about the entire history of Western civilization) in his work, with a sense of completeness about the finished form, Powys's work for all its massiveness manages to leave out more than it puts in. *Ulysses* tries to capture eternity in a drop; *A Glastonbury Romance* is a plunge in the ocean, and no matter how much we swim in it, we can only experience a fraction of the totality. Yet admitting the latter's sprawling form and its less precise use of language, it is an adventure to read. There is a Lawrencian vitality in Powys's characters, an intensity of naked feeling that compares to Dostoevsky, against a Tolstoian panoramic sweep of life.

The scene is Glastonbury, center of many Arthurian legends, a place that evokes the Camelot of myth. Local landmarks are associated with such things as King Arthur's tomb and the lake where he obtained the magic sword Excalibur. But the dominant symbol in the book, the goal of Arthur's quest and of the lives of the characters here, is the Holy Grail.

John Geard, a former evangelistic preacher and secretary to the late Canon William Crow, unexpectedly inherits the old man's fortune. Philip Crow, the Canon's nephew and prominent Glastonbury industrialist, is infuriated at having been deprived of what he feels is his rightful estate. Geard is odd-looking: he has a robust body but the head of a hydrocephalic dwarf, and he intends to use his new wealth to establish Glastonbury as a spiritual center of the world.

In a fortuitous stroke, he is elected mayor of Glastonbury and gains freedom to pursue his plans. He stages a passion play that incorporates the Arthurian legends and the older Welsh myths of Merlin with the traditional story of Christ's crucifixion. Later on Chalice Hill, associated by legend with the Grail, he erects a "Saxon Arch" over a path leading to a "Grail Spring." There Geard performs miracles: he cures a woman dying of cancer, he restores a dead child to life. He holds forth daily on his new religion to crowds of admiring pilgrims.

Despite Philip's powerful opposition, the communists who have supported Geard's election turn Glastonbury into a commune. Its economy prospers under the new system due to the influx of pilgrims, while Philip suffers setbacks in his great ventures, a tin mine and a dyeworks. Philip's own kin turn against him as well: his cousin John Crow becomes Geard's chief organizer for the pageant; his cousin Mary aligns herself with John and eventually marries him; while cousin Persephone and her husband Dave, inveterate communist organizers, stir up trouble among Philip's workers.

The efforts of capitalist and communist alike are washed away in the end, however, when a huge flood overwhelms Glastonbury. Geard himself drowns—albeit quite willingly—while saving Philip, who remains unimpressed by the sacrifice. Geard gains a last vision of the Grail, "that nameless Object, that fragment of the Absolute, about which all his days he had been murmuring," and thus dies fulfilled.[27]

It is impossible to convey the intricacy of the relationships between characters in this novel by any summary, for all forty-eight of them seem somehow crucial to the whole. The opposition between good and evil, or creation and destruction, goes on not only between characters but inside each of them, just as it goes on inside the cosmic source of all life, which Powys refers to as the "First Cause." A strange democracy of souls exists in which the heroic and the petty alike achieve an ennobled equivalency, like waves on an ocean. This feature perhaps accounts for the work's apparent lack of form. One cannot easily grasp the whole through one of its parts.

This unorthodox structure requires a nonlinear model to follow. I have given some main lines of the linear, conventional plot structure that can be discerned, and Glen Cavaliero has done this in more detail, dividing the novel into six main sections but asserting that its primary mode of development is pictorial rather than dramatic.[28] In my view this pictorial design, or whatever we want to call it, can be vindicated by considering the form as a reflection of the purpose of the book.

Powys, in his preface to the novel, states that he attempted to describe "Nothing more and nothing less than the effect of a particular legend, a special myth, a unique tradition, from the remotest past in human history, upon a particular spot on the surface of this planet together with its inhabitants of every age and of every type of character."[29] Unifying the variety is the symbol of the Grail, which only a few characters consciously cognize, but which affects everyone's actions from behind the scenes. It represents an archetypal force, the Eternal Feminine, the vessel into which the Fountain of Life is poured. Powys says that the novel's message "is that no one Receptacle of Life and no one Fountain of Life poured into that Receptacle can contain or explain what the world offers us."[30] This may be why reading him is like swimming on one shore of a vast ocean. There is always the sense of greater expanses of ocean beyond the horizon. The work itself is a Grail, a receptacle filled to overflowing—which, like the culminating flood, carries us away outside its time and space. We realize we have been shown only a tiny fraction of what is there, and that in spite of eleven hundred pages crowded with incident and detail and ideas, Powys has restrained himself.

Unity consciousness is the perception of the Absolute in the relative, and in order to give a vision of Unity, the novel takes a "pictorial" form. Powys stresses the immanence of the Grail in every event down to the most mundane. Every event is elevated to absolute significance. The relative values still persist: that is, we can assign an importance to some events over others if we choose, and designate some characters as major and others as minor, but always the absolute dimension is primary. This is consistent with the nature of Unity consciousness, in which relative distinctions are not eliminated. Two people in Unity may certainly differ in their tastes and preferences even while sharing that highest level of consciousness. But underlying the field of change, the non-changing essence shines through equally, illuminating the entire fabric of relative perception and giving every event and person and object an absolute validity.

What seems formless in *A Glastonbury Romance,* then, is simply the vitality of Powys's vision overbrimming the artistic receptacle. He tries to convey the immanence of the higher order of the Absolute, finding it in the most ordinary occurrence. For example, at one point Owen Evans, a Welsh antiquary, experiences a wave of egocentric contemplation while sitting upon a turnip heap. At that very moment the First Cause gives itself up to the same egocentric impulse, as does a microscopic creature on the surface of the turnip Evans is eating. Everything in creation is connected, and the good or evil that displays itself in human action is part of a wave that extends from god to bug. We are constantly reminded that nature and human life are indissolubly linked. To look at another example, after the reading of the Canon's will, which excludes the Crows and causes bitter feelings, night brings a transcendental essence of normalization to the uneasy atmosphere of Canon Crow's house:

> Sweet-scented, obliterating, equalising, it flowed in, taking the bitterness from defeat, taking the triumph from victory, and diffusing through the air an essence of

something inexplicable, something beyond hope and beyond despair, full of pardon and peace.[31]

The main reason that the book is so long is that Powys keeps us informed of the psychic state of the environment and indeed of the cosmic intelligence behind it all.

Powys spends time on the intricate linkages between human consciousness and the consciousness in nature because he sees life as moving purposefully in an evolutionary direction, propelled by its own natural tendencies "towards some implied fulfilment in accordance with some deeply-involved entelechy."[32] In his own life Powys delineated five dominant tendencies: "a desire to enjoy the Cosmos, a desire to appease my Conscience, a desire to play the part of a Magician, a desire to play the part of a Helper, and finally a desire to satisfy my Viciousness."[33] Each of these desires points towards a fulfillment best expressed in the state of Unity consciousness, and each is an important theme in *A Glastonbury Romance*. I shall examine them one by one.

The desire to enjoy the cosmos is found particularly in John Geard, who has the "power of relaxing his whole being and enjoying physical sensations without the least self-consciousness or embarrassment in anyone's presence."[34] One of the best examples of this is a "heretical Easter mass" that he celebrates in solitude. He takes a loaf of bread and decanter of port wine, goes out in his garden early Easter morning, and squatting in the bushes falls on the flesh and blood of his Master with "ravenous greed," muttering "Christ is risen! Christ is risen!" The birds are hypnotized with amazement.[35] This ability is what Powys has called in his philosophical writings a "psychic-sensual ecstasy," which he sees as the end of life:

> What this psychic sensuous ecstasy that I am defending really implies is a direct embrace of life. It is, in fact, a sublimated synthesis of the sex-instinct, the hunger-instinct, the thirst-instinct. It is a see-hear-touch-taste-smell complex, with an overtone of psychic imagination. It corresponds in human beings to the enjoyment-feeling of trees, animals, birds, fishes, and reptiles. It gathers itself together, in a stoical defiance of discomfort and misery, and forces itself to breathe in, and to breathe out, the bitter-sweet air of universal life.[36]

Geard's apparently gross sensual indulgence thus has a spiritual element. The purpose of his mass is to contact the in-breathing, out-breathing current of universal life which vibrates in the elemental earth.

What Powys is advocating is not hedonism in the sense of a denial of all super-material values. He makes it clear in his *In Defence of Sensuality* that his "psychic-physical happiness" or "elementalism" is identical with the *agape* that Christ preached, especially in the Gospel of John (which is Geard's favorite).[37] This kind of enjoyment is akin to the nature of perception in Unity consciousness. Cosmic consciousness is the distinction between the self and non-Self and the prerequisite for ultimate enjoyment of the non-Self in terms of the Self. Powys recognizes the necessity for first establishing in solitude what the Self is: the "I am I," detached from the world, and having nothing to do with the body or with thoughts in the mind. From that standpoint we can "fling our spirit into the Inanimate" and recognize the Eternal culminating in every moment, in "lovely floating shapes that are as it were islands of infinity in the rushing sea of time. To isolate these moments, to arrest them and hold them and fuse our spirit with them is the real purpose of life."[38] Powys parts company with conventional Christianity because he finds it too otherworldly. It denies the fusion of spiritual and physical appreciation that is possible on this earth. But the essence of Christianity is preserved in the Grail, "a morsel of the Absolute and a broken-off fragment of the First Cause."[39] It has long been a Christian symbol for the attainment of divine vision.

As the desire to enjoy the cosmos was Powys's own dominant wish, the character that most closely resembles him, John Crow, shares this instinct very strongly. Although Geard's right-hand man, John is a skeptic and is counted an enemy of the Grail. Yet because his nature leans towards psycho-sensual ecstasy (he worships stones and trees), and because his love relationship with Mary is vital and spontaneous, we are moved to agree with Geard's comment that John has "a good deal more religion than he thinks he has."[40] He refuses, whatever happens, to be unhappy, "which constituted in his mind the only morality."[41] Thus John Crow is as religious, in his fashion, as John Geard.

The second of Powys's "dominant tendencies," his desire *to appease his Conscience,* manifests most particularly in the characters of Mat Dekker, Vicar of Glastonbury, and his son Sam. Both are in love with Nell Zoyland, who is ambivalently unhappy with her husband Will. But whereas Mat has severely restrained himself from thinking of her romantically, Sam has won her heart and the two are conducting an affair at which Will winks cynically. Sam's loyalties are divided, however, between Nell and Christ. He is convinced that "possession" is a mortal sin that destroys happiness, and his conflict resolves itself into this form: "possessing Nell, or being possessed by Christ." Even after she becomes pregnant by him, he thinks: "A month-old conception, a year-old love, what were these beside the ecstasy, the blind exultation of sharing the sufferings of a God?"[42]

Sam's identification with the suffering Christ opposes Powys's conception of divinity incarnate, implied in the ecstatic psychic-sensuous experiences of those in the novel who perceive the Grail. Nell thinks it is the Devil, not Christ, who is tearing Sam from her. In a sense, it is the Devil in the form of Sam's isolate soul that is forcing his body to comply with its intense will to self-sacrifice. Powys analyzes this as a form of power-lust.

The conscientious impulses of both Mat and Sam to renounce Nell create great tension in them, which implies that what we call conscience may often be a kind of egoistic self-assertion of one aspect of the will over the more spontaneous and possibly more beneficent instinct. They prefer total renunciation of Nell and embrace their suffering as a virtue, rather than face the fact of their temptation and work through it.

Sam's dilemma is resolved happily. He breaks it off with Nell, goes to live by himself and work in a factory, and in this monastic-style withdrawal he learns to be strong in himself. He finally realizes that self-sacrifice has its limits: "Absolute sympathy with suffering would mean death. . . . If Christ had sympathized to the limit with the pain of the world it would have been hard to live until the day of his Crucifixion. . . . There comes a point when to live at all we must forget!"[43] He discovers the secret of matter: no longer is it inanimate, but "electric with animation." It assumes a cosmic shape: "Ichthus, the World Fish," an image of Christ as the indwelling soul of matter.[44] In a blinding vision of the Grail all his conflicts are relieved. Feeling at first as if a gigantic spear has struck into his bowels, he experiences "crashing pain":

> But when the vision appeared, and it came sailing into the midst of this bleeding darkness that was Sam's consciousness, healing everything, changing everything, each detail of what he saw he saw with a clearness that branded it forever upon his brain. He saw a globular chalice that

had two circular handles. The substance it was made of was clearer than crystal; and within it there was dark water streaked with blood, and within the water was a shining fish.[45]

Seeing the Grail, feeling the redeeming force within him and without him, bolstered now by the elemental Ichthus-Christ, he is ready for reconciliation with Nell. But it is too late; she has made up with her husband:

> His conscious mind was sad, even to the verge of a sort of inert despair, from this loss of Nell at the very moment when he was ready to live with her; but, below his conscious mind, stirring still in the depths of his being, was the feeling: "I can endure whatever fate can do to me, for I have seen the Grail!"[46]

We feel that despite the ironic outcome of this episode, Sam has attained a level of permanent happiness that puts such vicissitudes in the background.

In his *Autobiography* Powys says that conscience often opposed his desires to live solely in terms of "sensual-mystical sensations." The character of Sam Dekker may be an attempt to work out this opposition. Certainly Sam is at least as receptive as anybody else, even Geard, to the sensuous-mystical elements of life, but he has a fierce zeal for withdrawal from the worldly. He resolves the conflict by passing through an ascetic period that prepares him to live a life of spiritual and material integration. Perhaps the ultimate value of conscience in this case is not the egoism that passes for conscience but the primacy of pure consciousness (which is etymologically linked, after all, with "conscience") as the basis for the sensuous enjoyment of Unity consciousness. The "I am I," or Self, realized in solitude by an act of detachment from the relative world, must be established in cosmic consciousness as co-existent with perception, thought, and action, before the eternal can be revealed as immanent in the outside world.

Powys's third dominant tendency, *to play the part of a Helper,* is reflected very strongly in Sam and Geard, who have a genuine and unforced spirit of generosity. By way of contrast, the communist Dave Spear's helping instinct is based on abandoning, for the sake of a cause, the vital principle of individual integrity. In his self-righteousness he claims that one can be "unimaginative, undistinguished, lacking in all sense of humor"—even be "inhuman"—if only one acts in accordance with the revolutionary imperative of communism. Spear's overweening confidence breaks down in a pub where he exhorts a crowd of workingmen, his "Comrades," to listen to his "voice of the Future." He opposes Geard's spiritual revival in favor of "the great spirit of life" which will melt the gravestone of Christ and Arthur in "one Sea, one Flood, one great calm . . . and quiet . . . and peace."[47] He then dissolves in a flood of tears, a presage of the great flood that is soon to bring an end to the Glastonbury communal experiment. Spear's idealism has no basis in a conviction of individual integrity, but rather it reflects a desire for oblivion and an end to the dynamics of opposition and progress that evolve better societies.

The true Helper in Powys seems to be the individual who, secure in his integrity, acts to help another. It involves not so much self-sacrifice in the ordinary sense, but rather a calling forth of all of one's inner resources of will, concentration, and power, commanded in an assertive spirit towards the welfare of another. Geard's cure of the cancer patient Tittie Petherton results from his assumption of the role of a "supernatural being," one who can tap the creative power of the first cause, and then direct that energy through the "spear" of his thoughts to destroy the cancer.[48] In helping another, the Helper helps himself, achieving a kind of apotheosis. The Helper acts as a person in Unity consciousness, perceiving the incursion of the invincible power of the Timeless into time and learning to harness that power.

Powys's desire *to satisfy his Viciousness* is reflected principally in the character of Owen Evans, who is tormented by fantasies of sadism and turns them against himself during the pageant, in which he enacts the role of Christ on the cross. Identifying himself even more than does Sam with the delusory ideal of the suffering Christ, he hears the inner cry of his soul—whether of God or Devil he cannot decide—which seems to mock him with the prospect of eternal damnation. Evans calls for a flood, as does Spear, to drown forever the "itching, biting, stinging, scorpion-lusts in smooth, deep fathoms of oblivious water,"[49] rather than prolonging the cruel ideal of redemption through suffering.

The desire for oblivion, to drown suffering in unconsciousness, is the very opposite of Geard's ideal of becoming fully conscious even to the point of consciously enjoying one's own death. Powys subscribed to the Heraclitean idea that "we learn to keep our inmost being in a fighting mood of tension between opposites"[50]—which is what Evans in his escapist tendencies failed to do. Evans recognized that there is a dialectic of creative and destructive forces operating within the human psyche, but still he could not accept the presence of negativity though he knew that without it "the whole teeming ocean of life would dry up."[51] This spiritual timidity eventually leads to the perverse embracing of that destructive element that has been avoided. Evans yearns to glut his sadistic impulses by secretly watching Finn Toller crush John Crow's skull with an iron bar. He is deterred from this sin at the last moment by his wife Cordelia, who manages to transform his perverted eroticism into normal sexual desire for her. John Crow, who escapes his assassin, also has a "vicious" streak, but he quenches it in lovemaking with Mary. In both cases, woman is the means for men's salvation from their self-destructive impulses. An incarnation of the elemental life of the female Earth, she is a bearer of the Grail, which can receive all the sweet and bitter waters of pent-up passion.

We might regard the tendency towards "viciousness" as that imbalance in human nature of negative over positive energies. In the despair over trying to cast off the negative, one becomes destructive towards both self and others. Forgetting that the purpose of life is happiness, one willfully suffers to punish oneself, whereas only in the release of "psychic-sensuous ecstasy" is freedom from the negative imbalance possible. The will to suffer resists acceptance of the solitary "I am I," the integrated subjective state that precedes the reverent, sensuous embrace of the cosmos in Unity consciousness.

Powys's desire *to play the role of Magician* is embodied in Geard, who in his miracles follows the precedent of Merlin and Christ. Accused of perpetrating lies, he responds:

> "I tell you, *any lie* as long as a multitude of souls believes it and presses that belief to the cracking point, *creates new life,* while the slavery of what is called truth drags us down to death and to the dead! Lies, magic, illusion— these are names we give to the ripples on the water of our experience when the Spirit of Life blows upon it. . . . Miracles are lies; and yet they are happening. Immortality is a lie; and yet we are attaining it. Christ is a lie; and yet I am living in him."[52]

Because he has the ability to appreciate the soul in matter, to see the universe as alive, the true magician can destroy and build it up as he chooses. Every person's picture of the world is a magical construction, a tissue of lies that may be real enough for him but invalid for anybody else. Unlike the wretched man who is miserable with the world he has created, the Magician knows that he can change that which consists, after all, of the stuff of his own consciousness. If he doesn't like the lie he is living, then he picks a better one.

The *maya,* or world-illusion of Indian philosophy, is the reality of perception in Unity consciousness. From that level "life is a dream," as Calderón tells us, but a dream which we can shape to our ends for the greater happiness of ourselves and others. At one point the realization comes to John Crow that he need not be trapped in his dream:

> Pain was real—that woman crying out upon her cancer and calling it "Lord! Lord!"—but even pain, and all the other indescribable horrors of life seemed, as he stared at the backs of those moving sheep, to be made of a "stuff," as Shakespeare calls it, that could be compelled to yield, to loosen, to melt, to fade, under the right pressure.[53]

The ultimate magic trick is to reach the state of consciousness whereby matter becomes malleable, porous, flexible, so that one is its master and not its slave. This is better than any objectively verifiable "miracle." In Powys's words, "What is a magician if not one who converts God's 'reality' into his own 'reality.' God's world into his own world, and God's nature into his own nature?"[54]

We have seen that different characters in the story reflect Powys's personal preoccupations, and that the patterns of the characters' inner and outer conflicts are quite complex. In view of the muddiness of some of this complexity it might seem paradoxical to discuss the book in terms of Unity consciousness. Indeed, Powys often speaks in his philosophical writings of the "pluralistic" nature of the universe "wherein an assemblage of bodies and souls, some visible, some invisible, struggle for their own individual vision."[55] *All* matter, for Powys, has a body and soul: the universe is composed of infinite individual consciousness, and even the First Cause of all creation is not unitive, it is a dual current of creation and destruction. All good and all evil emanate from it. Nevertheless, Powys's emphasis on the search for "the constant enjoyment . . . which constitutes the only indestructible ecstasy of life" qualifies his vision as corresponding to Unity; for only in Unity consciousness does one enjoy the infinite complexity of the relative in its eternal and non-changing value.

Still, it must be admitted that Powys specifically denied subscribing to the Hindu "pantheistic" idea of identifying the "I am I" with the universe:

> In [the Hindu] system, the *this* and the *that* become one. To any Nordic mind, however, it seems much wiser to keep the "this" and the "that" firmly and clearly apart, and to allow every self to satisfy its egotism by isolating itself from the universal.[56]

Powys somehow developed a subtle misunderstanding of the philosophy of Unity consciousness spoken of in the Upanishads, for cosmic consciousness, the state of separation of "this" and "that," which he praises in this passage, precedes Unity in the evolution of consciousness but its values are by no means destroyed by the attainment of the higher state. Cosmic conscousness prepares the way for the ultimate ecstasy—the appreciation of all "this" phenomenal world in terms of "that" absolute reality. Even in Unity, the distinction between Absolute and relative is not entirely lost. We can learn that both water vapor and ice are nothing other than water without losing the ability to distinguish between the two. Duality and Unity can coexist.

Powys's conception of a dualistic First Cause might seem incompatible with a holistic picture of the universe. But many religions associate both creative and destructive powers with the highest deity, and for Powys, God's "evil" is merely a synonym for the primal destructive force. A human life becomes "evil" when destructiveness gains an unnatural supremacy over the good or creative power, but to get rid of the destructive potential altogether would be to eliminate the possibility for evolution and progress in life. This, no doubt, is why Powys sees "evil" as innate in the Supreme Being.

Powys emphasizes creation, however, not destruction. The conclusion of the novel is a paean to the earth goddess Cybele, whose spirit he praises for ever thrusting her Turrets of the Impossible into the lives of those that will receive her:

> For She whom the ancients named Cybele is in reality that beautiful and terrible Force by which the Lives of great creative Nature give birth to Truth that is to be.

Out of the Timeless she came down into time. Out of
the Un-named she came down into our human symbols.

Through all the stammerings of strange tongues and
mutterings of obscure invocations she still upholds her
cause; the cause of the unseen against the seen, of the
weak against the strong, of that which is not, and yet is,
against that which is, and yet is not.

Thus she abides; her Towers forever rising, forever
vanishing. Never or Always.[57]

Powys insists on a fulfillment in terms of the physical, in terms of humanity's union with physical nature, and it is appropriate that he should
invoke the Eternal Feminine with its traditional association with the
created physical universe of Maya. But he recognizes that this ultimate
state of Unity can only be gained after an individual is established in
the Self—the "I am I" of cosmic consciousness. The narrowly
"spiritual" life of asceticism is to him an avoidance of the physical
which it is our destiny to embrace in total appreciation. But of the union with the "forever rising, forever vanishing" eternal beauty incarnate
in the flux of nature, only one living in the solitude of pure consciousness can know.

Chapter 7

THE ENLIGHTENED ARTIST

This universe is a tree eternally existing, its roots aloft, its branches spread below. the pure root of the tree is Brahman, the immortal, in whom the three worlds have their being, whom none can transcend, who is verily the Self.[1]

In this quotation from the Katha Upanishad, the Tree is an archetypal image of the cosmos. Few things in nature are so suggestive of both stability and flexibility, of organization and asymmetry, of simplicity and complexity. Its roots are in the unseen—as if unmanifest—basis of the visible manifest form. A tree is a universe unto itself, and it harmonizes the opposites of life. It is a living symbol of wholeness.

Rilke's exclamation, "A tree inside the ear!" is his recognition that man also is a microcosm and contains within him the whole universe. He echoes the ancient adage, "As above, so below"; that is, we as humans are composed of the same orderliness and measure that we perceive "above" in the objective creation. This is the reality of the state of consciousness called Unity. The Self overflows the bounds of subjectivity and permeates the fabric of the external universe, investing all animate and inanimate creation with living, pulsing cosmic intelligence.

When one person achieves enlightenment, all others benefit regardless of their own state of consciousness. The qualities of a great man or woman resonate through thoughts, actions, speech, gestures, smiles to everything and everybody. We are all uplifted by that uplifted vision. We can feel concretely how the quality of that consciousness affects our own.

The Upanishadic tree in the quotation is upside down because its branches constitute the multifarious networks of relative life in which humanity is always playing. If we are confined to those branches then we are truly on the lesser evolved levels of consciousness. But as we ascend the inverted tree, the diversity is unified in the main trunk. Finally we reach the "pure root," or transcendental level that sustains relativity. Brahman is the name given to the full range of life, both absolute and relative, and the image of the tree encompasses it all.

Many artists have no doubt experienced transcendental consciousness and higher states; others have had only an intuitive understanding about them. I have not attempted to make any judgments about the authors discussed in this book; it is impossible to evaluate other people's state of consciousness on the basis of what they do, say, or write. We may infer from their work a sense of, say, cosmic consciousness, but this does not mean that the artist was fully enlightened. It is possible to have flashes of higher states, even Unity, long before one is fully established in cosmic consciousness. Throughout the ages, all kinds of people have had such flashes; some have been recorded, most not. In addition to scriptures, it is the artists who have through their works most often reminded us of the possibilities for higher perception and integration of life.

As deep-running roots are necessary for a tree to fully flower, so higher consciousness is a requirement of truly great art. As Maharishi says:

> If the artist is really living Being, Infinity, his piece of art will speak of maximum value of life. Most enlivened will be that piece of art and as such it will last longer in time. So the artist, just as he promotes life into the lifeless, promotes eternity in time. And this is possible on the basis of living fullness of life: how much the Self, eternal infinite being . . . speaks in the strokes of the artist, how much the artist vibrates in that value of infinity, how much the artist vibrates Being in that value of Being— that much will the stroke vibrate into the value of life.[2]

Maharishi continues that the artist must be the person of fully-developed mind and heart, and that through meditation that integrative ideal becomes a practical goal.

The question might arise: when the artist achieves enlightenment, will he need to create? If he were perfect in himself, would not the creative urge, indeed the urge to do anything, subside? Quite to the contrary. The artist's happiness does not prevent him from working, for the work emerges from him out of necessity. It *happens* to him, though of course the birth must be actively encouraged and directed. A creative effort is like sailing: it takes training, skill, and practice to align the sail and tiller, but the source of power is far beyond anything the sailor could muster. The artist's joy in cooperating with that power should not be supplanted by the inner peace which comes with higher consciousness.

The will to create is as inexorably a part of the artist's nature as the earth's need to grow flowers in the spring. The misconception that man is separate from nature has led to the idea that his creative activity is artificial or inferior, but there is no essential difference between creative intelligence as it manifests in nature and in man. The writing of *The Divine Comedy* is lesser in scale than the creation of the world, but the principle is the same.

In enlightenment the will is said to be "free" at last. Free will and universal will are really two aspects of the same thing, just as particles and waves are two different but equally valid ways of describing the nature of light. As Anthony Campbell points out, in cosmic consciousness life becomes completely paradoxical, as both the full scope of the free will and the all-pervasiveness of predestination are realized clearly:

> In cosmic consciousness one perceives that action depends on impersonal forces (the laws of nature) but one also perceives that one's Self is not involved with this play of forces; hence one is free. Thus it could be said that in the state of ignorance the free will paradox is in solution, detectable only by intellectual analysis, whereas in cosmic consciousness it has visibly crystallized out and cannot be missed.[3]

In Unity consciousness all potential viewpoints are encompassed by the unitive vision in which the two most fundamental opposites, absolute and relative, are one and the same. In Unity, the Self assumes the role of the universal will that flows through the world, and there is no longer an ultimate distinction between Self and Other. There is only Self, enlivening the tree of Being with the joyous flowers of creation.

In his poem "Among School Children," W. B. Yeats invokes the image of a chestnut tree, "great-rooted blossomer," and asks "Are you the leaf, the blossom or the bole?"

> O body swayed to music, O brightening glance,
> How can we know the dancer from the dance?[4]

Beneath the great tree of Being, consciousness is both the dancer and the dance. That is the ultimate vision of Unity to which we all may aspire.

NOTES

Chapter 1: Invitation to the Dance

1. Maharishi Mahesh Yogi, *Bhagavad-Gita: A New Translation and Commentary: Chapters 1 to 6* (1967; rpt. Baltimore: Penguin, 1969), p. 120.
2. Aniela Jaffé, ed., *Memories, Dreams, Reflections,* by C. G. Jung (New York: Random House, 1961), p. 335.
3. Jung, *Memories,* p. 393.
4. Joseph Campbell, *The Hero with a Thousand Faces,* 2nd ed. (Princeton, N. J.: Princeton Univ. Press, 1968), p. 30.
5. Campbell, p. 246.
6. Campbell, p. 386.

Chapter 2: Absurdity

1. Joseph Campbell, *Creative Mythology* (New York: Viking, 1961), p. 5.
2. Samuel Beckett, *Waiting for Godot* (New York: Grove, 1954), p. 39.
3. Beckett, p. 40.
4. Beckett, p. 51.
5. Beckett, p. 57.
6. Beckett, p. 34.
7. Samuel Beckett and Georges Duthuit, "Three Dialogues," in *Samuel Beckett: A Collection of Critical Essays,* ed. Martin Esslin (Englewood Cliffs, N.J.: Prentice-Hall, 1965), p. 17.
8. Luigi Pirandello, *Six Characters in Search of an Author,* trans. Edward Storer, in *Naked Masks: Five Plays,* ed. Eric Bentley (New York: Dutton, 1952), p. 218.
9. Pirandello, p. 266.
10. Pirandello, p. 235.
11. Quoted in Walter Starkie, Luigi Pirandello (Berkeley: Univ. of California Press, 1965), p. 46.

12. "Is There Room for 'Grace' in Buddhism?" in *The Sword of Gnosis: Metaphysics, Cosmology, Tradition, Symbolism*, ed. Jacob Needleman (New York: Penguin, 1974), p. 206.
13. Starkie, p. 44.
14. Pirandello, p. 218.
15. Starkie, p. 48.
16. Strindberg, *A Dream Play*, trans. Evert Sprinchorn (New York: Avon, 1974), p. 137.
17. Maharishi Mahesh Yogi, *Bhagavad-Gita*, p. 281.
18. Strindberg, p. 33.
19. Birgitta Steene, *The Greatest Fire: A Study of August Strindberg* (Carbondale: Southern Illinois Univ. Press, 1973), p. 99.
20. Strindberg, p. 132.
21. Strindberg, p. 25.

Chapter 3: Transcendence

1. Maharishi Mahesh Yogi, *Bhagavad-Gita*, pp. 99–102.
2. Ingmar Bergman, *The Seventh Seal*, in *Four Screenplays of Ingmar Bergman*, trans. Lars Malstrom and David Kushner (New York: Simon and Schuster, 1960), p. 159.
3. Bergman, pp. 162–163.
4. Bergman, p. 163.
5. Walt Whitman, "Song of Myself," in *Complete Poetry and Selected Prose*, ed. James E. Miller, Jr. (Boston: Houghton, 1959), p. 29 (Pt. VI).
6. Birgitta Steene, "*The Seventh Seal*: An Existential Vision," in *Focus on* The Seventh Seal, ed. Birgitta Steene (Englewood Cliffs, N.J.: Prentice-Hall, 1972), p. 94.
7. Bergman, p. 138.
8. Lawrence, *Apocalypse* (1931; rpt. New York: Viking, 1960), pp. 96–97.
9. Lawrence, p. 100.
10. Jung, *Memories*, pp. 32–33.
11. Jung, p. 45.
12. Jung, p. 42.
13. Jung, p. 225.
14. Jung, p. 291.
15. Jung, p. 293.
16. Jung, pp. 295–296.

17. Jung, p. 166.
18. Jung, p. 3.
19. Titus Burkhardt, "Cosmology and Modern Science," in *The Sword of Gnosis*, pp. 153–178.
20. Laurens van der Post, *Jung and the Story of Our Time* (New York: Random House, 1975), p. 154.
21. Jung, p. 337.
22. Maharishi Mahesh Yogi, *The Science of Being and Art of Living* (Los Angeles: International SRM Publications, 1966), pp. 271–281.
23. Jung, *Answer to Job*, 2nd ed. (Princeton, N. J.: Princeton Univ. Press, 1969), p. 108.
24. Thomas Pynchon, *The Crying of Lot 49* (1966; rpt. New York: Bantam, 1967), p. 10.
25. Pynchon, p. 69.
26. Pynchon, pp. 106–107.
27. Pynchon, p. 91.
28. Pynchon, p. 93.
29. Pynchon, p. 134.
30. Pynchon, p. 135.
31. Pynchon, pp. 137–138.
32. Pynchon, p. 62.
33. Pynchon, p. 13.
34. Maharishi Mahesh Yogi, *Bhagavad-Gita*, pp. 119–120.

Chapter 4: Enlightenment

1. Maharishi Mahesh Yogi, *Bhagavad-Gita*, p. 145.
2. Robert Bly, trans., *Lorca and Jiménez: Selected Poems* (Boston: Beacon, 1973), p. 77.
3. J. B. Trend, trans., *Juan Ramón Jiménez: Fifty Spanish Poems* (Oxford: Dolphin, 1950), p. 43.
4. Trend, p. 47.
5. H. R. Hays, trans., *Selected Writings of Juan Ramón Jiménez* (New York: Grove, 1957), p. 148.
6. Hays, p. 246.
7. Bly, p. 63.
8. Bly, p. 93.
9. Hays, pp. 242–243.
10. Bly, p. 73.

11. Bly, p. 85.
12. Hays,. p. 15.
13. Bly, p. 15.
14. Hays, p. 103.
15. Hays, pp. 215–216.
16. Hays, p. 83.
17. Faubion Bowers, *The New Scriabin: Enigmas and Answers* (New York: St. Martin's, 1973), p. 204.
18. Bowers, p. 147.
19. Scriabin, "The Poem of Ecstasy," trans. Faubion Bowers, Jacket Notes, *The Poem of Ecstasy and Prometheus, the Poem of Fire*, cond. Eugene Ormandy, Philadelphia Orchestra, RCA Victor, LSC-3214, 1971.
20. Scriabin, in Bowers, *New Scriabin*, p. 118.
21. Scriabin, in Bowers, *New Scriabin*, p. 190.
22. Lawrence, *The Escaped Cock* (1928; rpt. Los Angeles: Black Sparrow Press, 1973), p. 16.
23. *Escaped Cock*, p. 25.
24. *Escaped Cock*, p. 32.
25. *Apocalypse*, p. 59.
26. Maharishi Mahesh Yogi, *Bhagavad-Gita*, p. 340.
27. *Escaped Cock*, p. 21.
28. *Escaped Cock*, p. 54.
29. *Escaped Cock*, p. 57.
30. Lawrence, "Aristocracy," in his *Phoenix II: Uncollected, Unpublished, and Other Prose Works*, ed. Warren Roberts and Harry T. Moore (New York: Viking, 1968), p. 482.

Chapter 5: Celebration

1. Anthony Campbell, *Seven States of Consciousness: A Vision of Possibilities Suggested by the Teaching of Maharishi Mahesh Yogi* (New York: Harper, 1974), pp. 95–96.
2. All quotations from *The Bridge* from *The Complete Poems and Selected Letters and Prose of Hart Crane*, ed. Brom Weber (Garden City, N.Y.: Anchor-Doubleday, 1966), pp. 43–117.
3. R. W. B. Lewis, *The Poetry of Hart Crane: A Critical Study* (Princeton, N. J.: Princeton Univ. Press, 1967), p. 374.
4. *Blake: Complete Writings*, ed. Geoffrey Keynes (New York: Oxford Univ. Press, 1966), p. 433.

5. Blake, p. 617.
6. Crane, p. 221.
7. Sonnets I: 1, 5, 6, 7, in *Ten Sonnets to Orpheus,* trans. Robert Bly (Mudra/Zephyrus Image Magazine, 1972); others in *Duino Elegies and The Sonnets to Orpheus,* trans. A. Poulin (Boston: Houghton, 1977).
8. *Creating an Ideal Society: A Global Undertaking* (West Germany: MERU Press, 1976), pp. 76–77.
9. Rilke, *Letters to a Young Poet,* trans. M. D. Herder-Norton (New York: Norton, 1963), p. 34.

Chapter 6: Unity

1. *The Upanishads: Breath of the Eternal,* trans. Swami Prabhavananda and Frederick Manchester (1948; rpt. New York: Mentor, 1957), p. 70.
2. *Upanishads,* p. 91.
3. Robert M. Pirsig, *Zen and the Art of Motorcycle Maintenance* (New York: Bantam, 1975), p. 73.
4. Pirsig, p. 18.
5. Pirsig, p. 233.
6. Frank Budgen, *James Joyce and the Making of* Ulysses (Bloomington: Indiana Univ. Press, 1960), pp. 16–17.
7. Richard Ellmann, *Ulysses on the Liffey* (New York: Oxford Univ. Press, 1972), p. 30.
8. Rudolph Steiner, *The Gospel of St. John* (New York: Anthroposophic Press, 1962), p. 27.
9. Ellmann, p. 43.
10. James Joyce, *Ulysses* (New York: Random House, 1961), pp. 105–106.
11. Joyce, p. 783.
12. Joyce, p. 674.
13. Mircea Eliade, *Mephistopheles and the Androgyne: Studies in Relgious Myth and Symbol,* trans. J. M. Cohen (New York: Sheed and Ward, 1965), p. 105.
14. Joyce, p. 493.
15. Joyce, p. 782.
16. Joseph Campbell, *Hero,* p. 136.
17. Campbell, *Hero,* p. 162.
18. Joyce, p. 48.

19. Joyce, p. 164.
20. Joyce, p. 689.
21. Joyce, p. 698.
22. Joyce, p. 34.
23. Joyce, p. 734.
24. Harry Blamires, *The Bloomsday Book: A Guide Through Joyce's Ulysses* (London: Methuen, 1966), p. 245.
25. Joyce, p. 783.
26. John Cowper Powys, *A Glastonbury Romance* (1933; rpt. London: Pan, 1975), p. 21.
27. *Romance*, p. 1117.
28. Glen Cavaliero, *John Cowper Powys: Novelist* (Oxford: Clarendon, 1973), pp. 60–65.
29. *Romance*, p. xi.
30. *Romance*, p. xiii.
31. *Romance*, p. 66.
32. Powys, *Autobiography* (London: John Lane, The Bodley Head, 1934), p. 6.
33. *Autobiography*, p. 7.
34. *Romance*, p. 419.
35. *Romance*, p. 409–410.
36. Powys, *In Defence of Sensuality* (New York: Simon and Schuster, 1930), p. 182.
37. *Sensuality*, p. 40.
38. Powys, *A Philosophy of Solitude* (London: Jonathan Cape, 1933), p. 189–190.
39. *Romance*, p. 748.
40. *Romance*, p. 282.
41. *Romance*, p. 648.
42. *Romance*, p. 469.
43. *Romance*, p. 932.
44. *Romance*, p. 936.
45. *Romance*, p. 939.
46. *Romance*, p. 986.
47. *Romance*, pp. 1017–1018.
48. *Romance*, pp. 707–709.
49. *Romance*, p. 617.
50. *Solitude*, p. 41.
51. *Romance*, p. 349.
52. *Romance*, pp. 891–892.

53. *Romance,* p. 705.
54. *Autobiography,* p. 25.
55. *Sensuality,* p. 305.
56. *Sensuality,* p. 30.
57. *Romance,* p. 1120.

Chapter 7: The Enlightened Artist

1. *Upanishads,* p. 23.
2. Maharishi Mahesh Yogi, "Art and the Artist," lecture, Kossen, Austria, September, 1970.
3. Campbell, *Seven States of Consciousness,* p. 80.
4. *The Collected Poems of W. B. Yeats* (New York: Macmillan, 1970), p. 214.

BIBLIOGRAPHY

Alexander, Charles N., and Ellen J. Langer. *Higher Stages of Human Development: Perspectives on Adult Growth.* New York: Oxford University Press, 1990.

Beckett, Samuel, and Georges Duthuit. "Three Dialogues." In *Samuel Beckett: A Collection of Critical Essays.* Ed. Martin Esslin. Englewood Cliffs, N.J.: Prentice-Hall, 1965, pp. 16–22.

Beckett, Samuel. *Waiting for Godot.* New York: Grove, 1954.

Bergman, Ingmar. *The Seventh Seal.* In *Four Screenplays of Ingmar Bergman.* Trans. Lars Malmstrom and David Kushner. New York: Simon and Schuster, 1960, pp. 95–164.

Blake, William. *Complete Writings.* Ed. Geoffrey Keynes. New York: Oxford Univ. Press, 1966.

Blamires, Harry. *The Bloomsday Book: A Guide Through Joyce's Ulysses.* London: Methuen, 1966.

Bowers, Faubion. *The New Scriabin: Enigmas and Answers.* New York: St. Martin's, 1973.

Budgen, Frank. *James Joyce and the Making of* Ulysses. Bloomington: Indiana Univ. Press, 1960.

Campbell, Anthony. *Seven States of Consciousness: A Vision of Possibilities Suggested by the Teaching of Maharishi Mahesh Yogi.* New York: Perennial-Harper, 1974.

——————. *TM and the Nature of Enlightenment: Creative Intelligence and the Teachings of Maharishi Mahesh Yogi.* New York: Perennial-Harper, 1976.

Campbell, Joseph. *Creative Mythology.* New York: Viking, 1961.

——————. *The Hero with a Thousand Faces.* 2nd ed. Princeton, N.J.: Princeton Univ. Press, 1968.

Cavaliero, Glen. *John Cowper Powys: Novelist.* Oxford: Clarendon, 1973.

Coleridge, Samuel Taylor. *Biographia Literaria.* New York: Dutton, 1904.

Crane, Hart. *The Complete Poems and Selected Letters and Prose.* Ed. Brom Weber. Garden City, N.Y.: Anchor-Doubleday, 1966.

Creating a Global Society: A Global Undertaking. West Germany: MERU Press, 1976.

Eliade, Mircea. *Mephistopheles and the Androgyne: Studies in Religious Myth and Symbol.* Trans. J. M. Cohen. New York: Sheed and Ward, 1965.

Ellmann, Richard. *Ulysses on the Liffey.* New York: Oxford Univ. Press, 1972.

Goswami, Anit, with Richard E. Reed and Maggie Goswami. *The Self-Aware Universe: How Consciousness Creates the Material World.* New York: Tarcher/Putnam, 1993.

Grof, Stanislav, with Hal Zina Bennett. *The Holotropic Mind: The Three Levels of Human Consciousness and How They Shape Our Lives.* New York: HarperCollins, 1993.

Haney, William S. *Literary Theory and Sankrit Poetics: Language, Consciousness, and Meaning.* Lewiston, N.Y.: Edwin Mellen Press, 1993.

Jiménez, Juan Ramón. *Juan Ramón Jiménez: Fifty Spanish Poems.* Trans. J. B. Trend. Oxford: Dolphin, 1950.

————. In *Lorca and Jiménez: Selected Poems.* Trans. Robert Bly. Boston: Beacon, 1973.

————. *Selected Writings of Juan Ramón Jiménez.* Trans. H. R. Hays. New York: Grove, 1957.

Johnson, Courtney. *Henry James and the Evolution of Consciousness.* East Lansing: Michigan State Univ. Press, 1987.

Joyce, James. *Ulysses.* Rev. ed. New York: Random, 1961.

Jung, C. G. *Answer to Job.* Trans. R. F. C. Hull. 2nd. ed. Princeton, N. J.: Princeton Univ. Press.

————. *Memories, Dreams, Relections.* Ed. Aniela Jaffé. Trans. Richard and Clara Winston. New York: Random House, 1961.

Lawrence, D. H. *Apocalypse.* 1931; rpt. New York: Viking, 1960.

————. "Aristocracy." In his *Phoenix II: Uncollected, Unpublished, and Other Prose Works.* Ed. Warren Roberts and Harry T. Moore.

————. *The Escaped Cock.* 1928; rpt. Los Angeles: Black Sparrow Press, 1973.

Lewis, R. W. B. *The Poetry of Hart Crane: A Critical Study.* Princeton, N.J.: Princeton Univ. Press, 1967.

Maharishi Mahesh Yogi. "Art and the Artist." Lecture, Kossen, Austria, September, 1970.

—————. *Bhagavad-Gita: A New Translation and Commentary: Chapters 1 to 6.* 1967; rpt. Baltimore: Penguin, 1969.

—————. *The Science of Being and Art of Living.* Rev. ed. Los Angeles: International SRM Publications, 1966.

Needleman, Jacob, ed. *The Sword of Gnosis: Metaphysics, Cosmology, Tradition, Symbolism.* New York: Penguin, 1974.

Orme-Johnson, Rhoda. "A Unified Field Theory of Literature." *Modern Science and Vedic Science,* 1 (September 1987): 323–373.

Pirandello, Luigi. *Six Characters in Search of an Author.* Trans. Edward Storer. In his *Naked Masks: Five Plays.* Ed. Eric Bentley. New York: Dutton, 1952, pp. 211–276.

Pirsig, Robert M. *Zen and the Art of Motorcycle Maintenance.* 1974; rpt. New York: Bantam, 1975.

Powys, John Cowper. *Autobiography.* London: John Lane, The Bodley Head, 1934.

—————. *A Glastonbury Romance.* 1933; rpt. London: Pan, 1975.

—————. *In Defence of Sensuality.* New York: Simon and Schuster, 1930.

—————. *A Philosophy of Solitude.* London: Jonathan Cape, 1933.

Pynchon, Thomas. *The Crying of Lot 49.* 1966; rpt. New York: Bantam, 1967.

Rilke, Rainer Maria. *Duino Elegies and The Sonnets to Orpheus.* Trans. A. Poulin. Boston: Houghton, 1977.

—————. *Letters to a Young Poet.* Trans. M. D. Herder Norton. Rev. ed. New York: Norton, 1963.

—————. *Ten Sonnets to Orpheus.* Trans. Robert Bly. N.p.: Mudra/Zephyrus Image Magazine, 1972.

Scriabin, Alexander. "The Poem of Ecstasy." Trans. Faubion Bowers. Jacket Notes. *The Poem of Ecstasy and Prometheus, the Poem of Fire.* Cond. Eugene Ormandy, Philadelphia Orchestra. RCA Victor, LSC-3214, 1971.

Starkie, Walter. *Luigi Pirandello.* Berkeley: Univ. of California Press, 1965.

Steene, Birgitta, ed. *Focus on* The Seventh Seal. Englewood Cliffs, N.J.: Prentice-Hall, 1972.

—————. *The Greatest Fire: A Study of August Strindberg.* Carbondale: Southern Illinois Univ. Press, 1973.

Steiner, Rudolph. *The Gospel of St. John.* New York: Anthroposophic Press, 1962.

Strindberg, August. *A Dream Play.* Trans. Evert Sprinchorn. New York: Avon, 1974.

The Upanishads: Breath of the Eternal. Trans. Swami Prabhavananda and Frederick Manchester. 1948; rpt. New York: Mentor, 1957.

Van der Post, Laurens. *Jung and the Story of Our Time.* New York: Random, 1975.

Whitman, Walt. *Complete Poetry and Selected Prose.* Ed. James E. Miller, Jr. Boston: Houghton, 1959.

Wilber, Ken. *The Spectrum of Consciousness.* 2nd ed. Wheaton, Ill.: Quest Books, 1993.

Yeats, W. B. *The Collected Poems of W. B. Yeats.* New York: Macmillan, 1970.

INDEX

ABOUT THE AUTHOR

Douglas A. Mackey was born in Evanston, Illinois, in 1947. He graduated with honors in English from the University of Kansas in 1969, followed by an M.A. and Ph.D. in English from the same institution. His dissertation was on the poetry of D. H. Lawrence.

Mackey taught literature and writing at Maharishi International University in Fairfield, Iowa, from 1975–77. *The Dance of Consciousness* evolved from his teaching at that time. Subsequently he worked for the College Division of Little, Brown & Co., Publishers, and then as an editor and writer for Corporate Education Resources, Inc., and HRSoft, Inc.

His published books include *The Rainbow Quest of Thomas Pynchon* (Borgo Press, 1980); *D. H. Lawrence: The Poet Who Was Not Wrong* (Borgo Press, 1986); *Philip K. Dick* (Twayne Publishers, 1988); *The Work of Ian Watson: An Annotated Bibliography and Guide* (Borgo Press, 1989); and *Doors into the Play: A Few Practical Keys for Theatricians* (co-authored with Sydney H. Spayde; Borgo Press, 1993). He has also edited several editions of *The Corporate University Guide to Management Seminars*, *The Evaluation Guide to Executive Programs*, and *The Evaluation Guide to Health and Wellness Programs*, published by The Corporate University Press.

He lives in Fairfield, Iowa, with his wife Sally Henderson.

www.ingramcontent.com/pod-product-compliance
Lightning Source LLC
Chambersburg PA
CBHW021335090426
42742CB00008B/612